The Great Unknown

ANTONIO ROYO MARÍN

THE
GREAT
UNKNOWN

THE HOLY SPIRIT AND HIS GIFTS

SOPHIA INSTITUTE PRESS
Manchester, New Hampshire

To the Immaculate Virgin Mary,
most faithful spouse of the Holy Spirit
and a perfect example of
perfection and holiness

Contents

The Great Unknown

Introduction

THE FIRST TIME St. Paul arrived in Athens, among the innumerable stone idols that filled the streets and squares and which prompted the satirist Petronius to say famously that "it is easier to meet a god than a man in this city,"[1] he was powerfully struck by an altar with the following inscription: "To the unknown God." This gave him the occasion for his magnificent speech in the Areopagus: "What therefore you worship as unknown, this I proclaim to you" (Acts 17:23).

Later, when the great apostle arrived again in the city of Ephesus, he found some disciples who had already accepted the Christian faith and asked them: "'Did you receive the Holy Spirit when you believed?' And they said, 'No, we have never even heard that there is a Holy Spirit'" (Acts 19:1–2).

Incredible as it may seem after twenty centuries, if St. Paul were to ask the same question again to a great multitude of Christians, he would obtain an answer very similar to the alarming one given by those first disciples in Ephesus. In any case, although His name may ring a bell, the vast majority of today's Christians know very little about Him.

---

[1] Petronius, *Satyricon*, 17.

3

We believe it is appropriate, first of all, to explain the main reasons and the sad consequences of this lamentable forgetfulness of the adored Person of the Holy Spirit.[2]

Lack of Demonstrations

The first reason for the general ignorance about the third Person of the Blessed Trinity is perhaps due to the fact that His manifestations are not very sensory and, therefore, often imperceptible to the vast majority of men.

The Father is well known, adored, and loved. How could it be otherwise? His works are evident and always present to our eyes. The magnificence of the heavens, the riches of the earth, the immensity of the oceans, the rush of the torrents, the roar of the thunder, the marvelous harmony that reigns throughout the universe, and a thousand other admirable things make apparent continuously, with sovereign eloquence and within the reach of all, the existence, the wisdom, and the formidable power of God the Father, Creator and Preserver of all that exists.

We also know, adore, and love immensely the Son of God. His preachers are no less numerous and eloquent than those of His Heavenly Father. The moving story of His birth, life, Passion, and death; the Cross, the temples, the images, the daily sacrifice of the altar, His numerous liturgical feasts that continually remind everyone of the different mysteries of His divine and human life; the Eucharist, above all, which perpetuates His real, though invisible, presence on this earth, and makes the worship of the whole Catholic Church converge toward Him.

But with the Holy Spirit things are very different. Although it is true that, as St. Basil admirably says, and as we shall see at length

---

[2] See A. Arrighini, *Il Dio ignoto: lo Spirito Santo* (Turin: Marietti, 1937). We gather here the main ideas of the introduction.

throughout these pages, "everything that the creatures of Heaven and earth possess in the order of nature and of grace comes from Him in the most intimate and spiritual way," the sanctification that He works in our souls and the supernatural life that He spreads everywhere are by no means beyond the perception of the senses.[3] Nothing is more visible than the creation of the Father and nothing more hidden than the action of the Holy Spirit.

On the other hand, the Holy Spirit was not incarnated like the Son. He did not live or converse visibly with men. Only three times has He manifested Himself under a sensible sign, but always secondary and passing: in the form of a dove over Jesus when He was baptized in the River Jordan, as a resplendent cloud on Mount Tabor, and as tongues of fire in the cenacle of Jerusalem. To this are reduced all His evangelical theophanies, and no other, it seems, has taken place throughout the history of the Church; wisely, the Church forbids itself to represent Him under any other symbol. The artists do not have here a variety of representative possibilities: only two or three symbols, and these very little human and not at all divine, are the only ones they can offer to the piety of the faithful to preserve the memory of His existence and His immense benefits.

Lack of Doctrine

Another reason for the great lack of knowledge of the Holy Spirit and His operations, among the faithful and the clergy alike, is the shortage of doctrine, due in turn to the scarcity of good publications, both ancient and modern, on the Divine Person Himself.

Bishop Gaume writes accordingly:

---

[3] St. Basil, *De Spiritu Sancto*, 29, 55.

How often have we heard our venerable brothers in the priesthood lament the lack of works on the Holy Spirit! Unfortunately, their lamentations are all too well founded. Indeed, what treatise on the Holy Spirit has been written in many centuries.... Even the teachings of classical theology on this subject are usually reduced to a few chapters of treatises on the Trinity, the Creed, and the sacraments. Everyone agrees that these notions are very insufficient. As for diocesan catechisms, which are necessarily even more restricted than the manuals of elementary theology, almost all are limited to a few definitions. One cannot but agree, with lively feeling, that even in the first Catholic nations the teaching on the Holy Spirit leaves much to be desired. Who would believe, for example, that among Bossuet's many sermons and panegyrics there is not even one on the Holy Spirit, not even one in Masillon, and hardly one in Bourdaloue?

It is true that the way to fill this lamentable gap would be to have recourse to the Fathers of the Church and to the great theologians of the Middle Ages, but who has the time and the ability to do so? From this comes an extreme difficulty for the zealous priest, both to instruct himself and to teach others.[4]

From the little that teachers generally know, one can deduce what the disciples will know. A few brief and abstract notions, which leave in the memory words rather than ideas, constitute the instruction of early childhood. On the occasion of Confirmation, it is true, these notions become a little more extensive and complete; but, on the

---

[4] J.-J. Gaume, *Treatise on the Holy Spirit*, (Barcelona: Agustín Jubera, 1885).

one hand, the still too tender age prevents the person from taking advantage of it and, on the other hand, one continues in the field of abstractions. Under the words of the catechist, the Holy Spirit does not take on body, does not become a person, God Himself; and not knowing what to say about His intimate nature, one goes on to speak of His gifts. But even these, being as they are purely spiritual and internal, are not accessible to the imagination or to the senses. Great, therefore, is the difficulty of explaining them, and greater still is the difficulty of making them understood. In ordinary teaching they are not clearly shown, neither in themselves, nor in their application to the acts of life, nor in their opposition to the seven deadly sins, nor in their necessary concatenation for the supernatural life of man, nor as the crowning of the edifice of salvation. For this reason, experience teaches that, of all the parts of Christian doctrine, the least understood and the least appreciated is precisely the one that should be most understood, since, and this is known and understood by everyone, to know little and poorly the third Person of the Most Holy Trinity is to know little and poorly this first and principal mystery of our holy faith, without which it is impossible to be saved.

Lack of Devotions

A third and serious reason combines with the preceding ones to maintain the lamentable state of affairs that we are denouncing: the scarcity of devotions, functions, and feasts around the Holy Spirit, while devotions multiply unceasingly on so many other things.

Certainly, all devotions approved by the Church are very useful and holy, and we have to admire and praise Divine Providence, which has been raising them up according to the various demands of religious and social life. Some of them are absolutely indispensable for the true Christian, such as the Passion of the Lord, the Blessed Sacrament, and the Virgin Mary. Jesus Himself and His

Holy Mother have been pleased to reveal to us the importance and advantages of some of these devotions relative to themselves, such as the Sacred Heart and the Most Holy Rosary. However, all this should not diminish or make us forget such an important and fundamental devotion as that of the Holy Spirit. This is the one that we must intensely foster, without diminishing those other devotions.

The feast of Pentecost itself, which in the liturgical rite is equal only to the most solemn feasts of Easter and Christmas, signifying the extraordinary importance that the Holy Church attaches to devotion to the third Person of the Most Holy Trinity, is not ordinarily celebrated with the splendor and enthusiasm that might be desired. While the other two solemnities of the liturgical year, Christmas and Easter, clearly show an adequate correspondence on the part of the faithful throughout the world, the Solemnity of Pentecost passes completely unnoticed, as if it were just any other Sunday. It is an indisputable fact that is repeated year after year.

In this way, almost the whole year goes by without a convenient celebration of the Holy Spirit.

Thoughtful Christians marvel and exasperate—rightfully so. The worst of all is that the great majority of the faithful do not even realize this great inconvenience and do not remember that in the God they worship there is a third Person called the Holy Spirit.

How could it be otherwise, when they hardly ever hear of this God, and never see Him appear on our altars? We can affirm it without rashness: for a great number of the faithful, the Holy Spirit is the unknown God of whom St. Paul found the altar when he entered Athens.

It should be noted, however, so as not to give rise to exaggerations or misunderstandings, that the Pauline formula "the unknown God," taken in its obvious sense, means not only that the pagans were completely ignorant of the existence of God, but that they did not have a correct idea of His perfections and works, and, above all, that they did not render Him the worship that was due to Him. Applied to the Holy Spirit, the formula "the unknown God" has nothing forced about it. According to St. Paul's concept, it means not so much that the Christians of our time are ignorant of the existence and divinity of the Holy Spirit, but that most of them do not have a sufficiently clear knowledge of His works, His gifts, His fruits, His sanctifying action in the Church and in souls, and, especially, they do not render Him the divine worship to which He is entitled, no less than the other two Persons of the Blessed Trinity. In this we believe that we can all agree.

Let us now look at the sad and pernicious consequences of such ignorance.

Fatal Consequences of This Oversight

From all that we have just said, it is evident that the Holy Spirit, as God, cannot experience any pain or sadness. Infinitely happy in Himself, He has no need of our remembrance or our homage. However, if He was able to experience pain, He could not help but experience it very intensely in the face of our incredible ignorance and forgetfulness of His Divine Person. He could repeat the same words that the psalmist puts into the mouth of the future Messiah abandoned by His beloved people: "Insults have broken my heart, so that I am in despair. I looked for pity, but there was none; and for comforters, but I found none" (Ps. 69:20).

This lament is all the more justified if we consider the pain, so to speak, that the Holy Spirit must experience in not being able to expand, as He ardently desires, over souls and over the Christian world. There is and can be nothing more diffusive than this divine Spirit, who is personally the supreme good; and yet, encountering the rebelliousness of our forgetful and indifferent freedom, He feels constrained to withdraw and restrict Himself, to limit His sanctifying action to very few souls who are entirely faithful to Him, to give as if with a miserly hand His ineffable gifts, since there are very few who ask Him for them and even fewer who are worthy of them. Moreover, He often sees those who are His temples of flesh and blood, those temples consecrated by Himself with the water of Baptism and sanctified and beautified in so many ways, miserably profaned with the foulest and most disgusting sins, and He sees Himself vilely cast out of these temples to give place to the spirit of fornication, hatred, revenge, pride, and all the other deadly sins.

Much more than the Holy Spirit Himself, Christians should be pained to see themselves so uninstructed and unworthy of such a great God. For this means, first of all, ignoring or despising the very source of supernatural and divine life.

The Church, in her fundamental Symbol, expressly attributes to the Holy Spirit this stupendous ability of conferring supernatural life on souls: "We believe in the Holy Spirit, Lord and giver of life" (*Dominum et vivificantem*). The dependence of supernatural life on the divine virtue of the Paraclete is a fundamental and eminently dynamic principle of Christianity. This principle, or rather, the practical orientation that derives from it, constitutes the starting point of all spiritual progress, of the progressive ascent from the common and simple Christian life to the highest and most sublime forms of holiness. It can be said that in this life-giving word, referring to the Holy Spirit, the whole theology of grace is enclosed as if it were a seed. It follows that, without an adequate knowledge and worship of the divine Spirit, the seed of Christian life, supernaturally infused by Him in Baptism, is paralyzed or hindered in its further development. The soul suffers, vegetates, and weakens, and it is very difficult for it ever to attain Christian life.

Those who do not care to know and adore the Holy Spirit—and unfortunately there are very many of them—place an insurmountable obstacle between Him and their supernatural life. This world of grace, this true and unique consortium of the soul with God, with all its divine elements, with its marvelous laws, with its sacred duties, with its incomparable magnificence, with its eternal reality, with its struggles, its joys, its alternatives, and its end; this superior world for which man has been created and in which he must live, move, and dwell, is as if it did not exist for him. The noble imitation which should spontaneously derive from all this is changed into cold indifference; esteem into contempt; love into disgust; enthusiasm into tedium and boredom. Created for Heaven, it seeks and appreciates nothing but the earthly, its life is concentrated in the sensible world and becomes purely earthly and animalistic. There is only one way to make it practical and profoundly Christian: to know, to invoke, to love, to live in intimate union with the Holy Spirit, Lord and giver of life: (*Dominum et vivificantem*).

We are therefore going to approach the theological-mystical study of the adored Person of the Holy Spirit and of His sanctifying action in the Church and in souls through His most precious gifts and charisms.

We offer these pages once again to the Immaculate Virgin Mary, most faithful spouse of the Holy Spirit, so that she may bless them and make them fruitful for the glory of God and the sanctification of souls.

Acronyms and Abbreviations

AAS Acta Apostolicae Sedis (Vatican City: 1909ff.).

ASS Acta Sanctae Sedis (Rome: 1865–1908).

Dz H. Denzinger (ed.), *Enchiridion symbolorum, definitionum et declarationum de rebus fidei et morum* (Freiburg: Herder, 1958).

PL J.-P. Migne (ed.), *Patrologiae Cursus completus. Series Latina*, 221 vols. (Paris: 1844–1879).

STh Summa Theologiae.

CHAPTER 1

The Holy Spirit in the Trinity

CATHOLIC DOCTRINE TEACHES us, as the first and most fundamental dogma of all, that there is only one God in three distinct
Persons: Father, Son, and Holy Spirit. This is clearly and explicitly
stated in divine revelation and has been infallibly proposed by the
Church in all the Symbols of the Faith. Because of its special ex-
plicitness and majestic rhythm, here we include the formulation of
the famous Athanasian Symbol Quicumque:

> Whoever wishes to be saved must first of all keep the
> Catholic faith; and whoever does not keep it intact
> and inviolate, will certainly perish forever.
>
> Now then: the Catholic faith is that we venerate
> one God in the Trinity, and the Trinity in unity;
> without confusing the Persons or separating the
> substance.
>
> For one is the Person of the Father, another of the
> Son, and another of the Holy Spirit; but the Father,
> the Son, and the Holy Spirit have one divinity, equal
> glory, and coeternal majesty.
>
> Such the Father, such the Son, such the Holy
> Spirit. Uncreated the Father, uncreated the Son, un-
> created the Holy Spirit.

Immense is the Father, immense is the Son, immense is the Holy Spirit.

Eternal is the Father, eternal is the Son, eternal is the Holy Spirit.

Yet they are not three eternal, but one eternal, just as they are neither three uncreated nor three immense, but one uncreated and one immense.

Likewise, omnipotent the Father, omnipotent the Son, omnipotent the Holy Spirit; and yet they are not three omnipotent, but one omnipotent.

Thus, God is the Father, God is the Son, God is the Holy Spirit: and yet they are not three gods, but one God.

Thus, Lord is the Father, Lord the Son, Lord the Holy Spirit; and yet they are not three lords, but one Lord; for, just as by Christian truth we are compelled to confess as God and Lord each particular Person, so the Catholic religion forbids us to say three gods and lords.

The Father was by no one made, nor created, nor begotten. The Son was by the Father alone, neither made nor created, but begotten. The Holy Spirit, of the Father and the Son, was not made, nor created, nor begotten, but proceeds.

There is, therefore, one Father, not three Fathers; one Son, not three Sons; one Holy Spirit, not three Holy Spirits.

In this Trinity, nothing is before or after, nothing greater or lesser, but the three Persons are co-eternal and co-equal. Therefore, as has been said above, in everything we must venerate the unity in the Trinity as much as the Trinity in unity.

Whoever, therefore, wants to be saved, must feel this way about the Trinity.

The Holy Spirit is, then, the third Person of the Most Holy Trinity, who proceeds from the Father and the Son, not by way of generation, as the Son is begotten by the Father, but by virtue of a mutual and ineffable current of love between the Father and the Son. Let us see, in a very brief summary, how the generation of the Word by the Father and the spiration of the Holy Spirit by the Father and the Son takes place in the bosom of the Most Blessed Trinity.

The Generation of the Son

Here is a simple popular exposition within everyone's reach:

> If one looks into a mirror, he produces an image similar to himself, for he resembles himself not only in figure, but also imitates his movements: if the man moves, his image moves also. This image, so similar, is produced in an instant, without work, without instruments and just by looking in the mirror. Thus we can imagine that God the Father, contemplating Himself in the mirror of His divinity with the eyes of His understanding and knowing Himself perfectly, engenders or produces an image absolutely equal to Himself. Now this image is the substantial figure of the Father, His perfect radiance, the total expression of the Father's intelligence, the subsistent and unique comprehensive word, the adequate term of the contemplation of the sovereign essence, the splendor of His glory and the image of His substance. He is, quite simply, His Son, His Word, the second Person of the Blessed Trinity.[5]

5   J. Miralles Sbert, quoted by A. Koch and A. Sancho, *Docete. Formación básica del predicador y del conferenciante*, (Barcelona: Herder, 1954), 21–27.

This generation is so perfect that it absolutely exhausts the infinite fruitfulness of the Father. Bossuet writes:

> God will never have another Son than this one, because He is infinitely perfect and there cannot be two like Him. One and only one generation of this perfect nature exhausts all His fruitfulness and attracts all His love. This is why the Son of God calls Himself the only one: *Unigenitus*, thus showing at the same time that He is Son not by grace or adoption, but by nature. The Father, confirming from on high this word of the Son, sends down from Heaven this voice: "This is my beloved Son, in whom I am well pleased. This is my Son, I have but Him, and from all eternity I have given Him and give Him all my love without ceasing."[6]

Monsignor Gay adds:

> Catholic theology teaches that God eternally enunciates Himself in a unique word, which is the very image of His being, the character of His substance, the measure of His immensity, the face of His beauty, the splendor of His glory. The life of God is infinite: millions of words uttered by millions of creatures, wisely discoursing about Him for millions of centuries, would not be enough to tell the story. This one Word says absolutely everything. He who would perfectly hear this Word, would understand all things; for He would understand the Author of things, and there would remain for Him no secrets in the divine nature,

---

[6] J. B. Bossuet, *Elevaciones del alma a Dios sobre los misterios de la religión christiana* (Madrid: Antonio Fernández, 1785), sem. 2.ª, elev. 1.ª.

but God alone eternally hears the Word that He pronounces. God speaks it; it speaks to God; it is God.[7]

For his part, Dom Columba Marmion expounds the divine generation of the Word in the following terms:

> It is marvelous what divine revelation reveals to us: in God there is fruitfulness, He possesses a spiritual and ineffable paternity. He is Father, and as such, the principle of all divine life in the Most Holy Trinity. God, infinite Intelligence, understands Himself perfectly. In a single act He sees all that is and all that is in Him; in a single glance He embraces, so to speak, the fullness of His perfections, and in a single idea, in a single word, which exhausts all His knowledge, He expresses that same infinite knowledge. That idea conceived by the eternal intelligence, that word by which God expresses Himself, is the Word. Faith also tells us that this Word is God, because He possesses, or rather, is with the Father, one and the same divine nature.
>
> Because the Father communicates to the Word a nature not only similar, but identical to His own, Sacred Scripture tells us that He begets Him, and therefore calls the Word the Son. The inspired books present us with the ineffable voice of God, who contemplates His Son and proclaims the Beatitude of His eternal fruitfulness: "From the womb of the morning like dew your youth will come to you" (Ps. 110:3); "Thou art my beloved Son; with thee I am well pleased" (Mark 1:11).

[7]   C. Gay, *Elevaciones sobre la gracia* (Madrid: San Lázaro, 1960) 1, 6.

17

This Son is perfect, possessing with the Father all the divine perfections, except the property of "being Father." In His perfection He is equal to the Father through unity of nature. Creatures can only communicate a nature similar to His: *simili sibi*. God begets God and gives Him His own nature, and, by the same token, He begets the infinite and contemplates Himself in another Person who is equal, and so equal, that both are one and the same thing, for they possess one divine nature, and the Son exhausts eternal fruitfulness; therefore He is one and the same thing with the Father: *Unigenitus Dei Filius ... Ego et Pater unum sumus* (see John 10:30).

Finally, that beloved Son, equal to the Father and yet distinct from Him and a divine Person like Him, is not separated from the Father. The Word always lives in the infinite Intelligence that conceives Him; the Son always dwells in the bosom of the Father who begets Him.[8]

The Procession of the Holy Spirit

Faith teaches us that the Holy Spirit, the third Person of the Blessed Trinity, proceeds from the Father and the Son by a sublime spiration of love. Here is a simple and popular exposition of the ineffable mystery:

> To understand this ineffable procession of love a little better, let us leave for a moment the divine metaphysics and simply question our heart, and it will tell us that its whole life consists in love.

8   Columba Marmion, *Jesucristo en sus misterios* (Barcelona: Editorial Litúrgica Española, 1941) 3, 1.

The heart beats continuously until it dies. In each beat it does nothing but repeat: I love, I love; that is my mission and my only occupation, and when it finally finds another heart that understands it and responds "I love you too," oh, what a great joy!

What is new between these two hearts to make them so happy, the mere movement of the heartbeats that seek and confuse each other? No. I am persuaded that between me and the one I love there is some *thing*. This thing cannot be my love, nor can it be her love; it is simply our love—that is to say, the marvelous result of the two heartbeats, the sweet bond that binds them together, the most pure embrace of the two hearts that kiss and intoxicate each other: our love. Ah, if only we could make it subsist eternally to testify, in a living and real way, that we have given ourselves totally and truly to each other! This fatal impotence, which, in human loves, always leaves a loophole for cruel uncertainties, can never occur in the heart of God.

Because God also loves, who can doubt it? He is precisely the substantial and eternal love: Deus caritas est (1 John 4:16).

The Father loves His Son: He is so beautiful! He is His own light, His own splendor, His glory, His image, His Word....

The Son loves the Father: He is so good, and gives Himself wholly and totally to Him in the generative act with such a kind and complete fullness!

These two immense loves of the Father and the Son are not expressed in Heaven with words, songs, shouts ... because love, reaching the highest degree, does not speak, does not sing, does not shout; but expands in a breath, in a breath, which between the

Father and the Son becomes, like them, real, substantial, personal, divine: the Holy Spirit.

Here then, with the heart, perhaps better than with metaphysical reasoning, the great mystery is revealed: the life of the Blessed Trinity, the generation of the Word by the Father and the procession of the Holy Spirit under the breath of their reciprocal love. In the life of the Trinity there is a continuous ebb and flow: the life of the Father, principle and source, overflows into the Son; and from the Father and the Son it is communicated, by way of love, to the Holy Spirit, the ultimate end of the intimate operations of the Divinity. This Holy Spirit, who thus enjoys the reciprocal gift of the Father and the Son, His consubstantial gift, gathers them together and maintains them, in turn, in unity. The three Persons, in possession of the one divine substance, are but one and the same, one true God.[9]

In more scientific language, but with identical doctrinal accuracy, Dom Columba Marmion explains the divine procession of the Holy Spirit as follows:

We know of the Holy Spirit only what revelation teaches us. What does revelation tell us? That He belongs to the infinite essence of one God in three Persons: Father, Son, and Holy Spirit. That is the mystery of the Holy Trinity. Faith appreciates in God the unity of nature and the distinction of Persons.

The Father, knowing Himself, enunciates and expresses this knowledge in an infinite word, the Word, with a simple and eternal act, and the Son, whom the

[9] A. Arrighini, *Il Dio ignoto*, w.c., 33–35.

Father begets, is similar and equal to Himself, because the Father communicates to Him His nature, His life, His perfections. The Father and the Son attract each other with mutual and unique love. The Father possesses such absolute perfection and beauty! The Son is such a perfect image of the Father! That is why they give themselves to each other, and this mutual love, which derives from the Father and the Son as from a unique source, is in God a subsistent love, a Person distinct from the other two, who is called the Holy Spirit. The name is mysterious, but revelation gives us no other.

The Holy Spirit is, in the interior operations of the divine life, the last term. He closes, if we are allowed to babble on about such great mysteries, the cycle of the intimate activity of the Most Holy Trinity. He is God the same as the Father and the Son, He possesses like them and with them the same and unique divine nature, the same science, the same power, the same goodness, the same majesty.[10]

This is what Catholic theology, relying immediately on the data of divine revelation, succeeds in telling us about the Holy Spirit in the bosom of the Most Blessed Trinity. Very little, certainly, but we do not know more. Only when the shadows of this mortal life are dissipated and the veil is drawn aside by means of the Beatific Vision will we contemplate with rapture the ineffable mystery, which will make the blessed dwellers of the heavenly Jerusalem eternally happy.

---

[10] Columba Marmion, *Jesucristo, vida del alma* (Barcelona: Editorial Litúrgica Española, 1955) I, 6, 1.

CHAPTER 2

The Holy Spirit In Sacred Scripture

AS WE HAVE already said in the previous chapter, we know nothing about the Holy Spirit and the other two divine Persons of the
Blessed Trinity apart from the data provided by divine revelation.
Natural reason, abandoned to its own forces, can demonstrate with
complete certainty the existence of God, deduced, by way of necessary causality, from the indisputable existence of created things.[11]
The clock inevitably claims the existence of the watchmaker.

The scientific demonstration of the existence of God also leads us
to the scientific knowledge of certain divine attributes, such as His
simplicity, immensity, goodness, eternity, infinite perfection, and
so on. In no way can it lead us to the knowledge of divine realities,
which surpass and transcend the way of natural knowledge that
man can obtain from the contemplation of created beings. Among
these infinitely transcendent truths is, in the first place, the ineffable
mystery of the Trinity of Persons in God. Without divine revelation,
natural reason would never have been able to suspect the existence
of three distinct Persons in the very simple unity of God.

---

[11] The First Vatican Council expressly defined it in the following words: "If
anyone should say that the one true God, our Creator and Lord, cannot
be known with certainty by the natural light of human reason by means
of the things that have been made, let him be anathema" (Dz 1806).

Let us see, then, what Sacred Scripture, which contains the treasure of divine written revelation, tells us about the Divine Person of the Holy Spirit. Let us see it, separately, in the Old and New Testaments.

Old Testament

In the Old Testament the Divine Person of the Holy Spirit does not appear with clarity and distinction, nor do those of the Father and the Son. However, there are many indications and traces that, in the light of the New Testament, appear as clear allusions to the Spirit of Love.[12]

The Hebrew expression *ruah Yahweh* (meaning spirit of God) appears in the Old Testament in various senses. There are four main groups that can be established:

1. First of all, it signifies the wind, by which God makes known His presence, His power, or His wrath. Thus it will appear even in the cenacle on the day of Pentecost.[13] It is also, from the beginning, the breath of life that God inspires in man and even in animals. When God withdraws it, death ensues, and if He gives it to the dead, they rise again.[14] Finally, in a broader sense, it is the creative breath, the wind of God that makes the world come out of nothing.[15]

2. Sometimes there are certain phenomena of a specifically religious character that are presented

---

[12] See *Iniciación teológica*, I (Barcelona: Herder, 1957) 421ff.
[13] See Gen. 3:8; Exod. 10:13,19; Exod. 14:21; Ps. 18:16; Acts 2:2.
[14] See Gen. 2:7; Gen. 7:15; Job 12:10; Job 34:14–15; Ps. 105:29–30; Ezek. 37:1–14; 2 Macc. 7:22–23.
[15] See Gen. 1:2; Ps. 33:6.

in very intimate dependence on the *ruah Yahweh*; such are, principally, the art of the workers
of the tabernacle, the power to govern the people received by Moses and transmitted by him
to the elders and Joshua, the warrior strength
and courage of the deliverers of Israel and,
above all, the prophetic inspiration. This is received individually or collectively, in a transitory or permanent way, with or without
external phenomena, by the leaders of the people and by the elders, or by individuals who do
not belong to the hierarchy; and it is transmitted by contagion or passed on.[16]

3. In a third group of texts, the *ruah Yahweh* is
shown to us as a breath of holiness. In the
Miserere of David, the expression "Holy Spirit"
appears for the first time. Its effects are stead-
fastness, good will, contrition and humility,
submission to God's will and the straightening
of our path, righteousness, justice and peace,
knowledge of the divine will and the gift of wisdom. The rebellious, on the other hand, those
who forge projects or establish covenants without this Spirit, accumulate sins upon sins and
distress the Holy Spirit of God.[17]

4. Finally, the *ruah Yahweh* is presented to us as an
essentially messianic phenomenon, first because

[16] See Exod. 31:3; Gen. 41:38; Num. 1:25; 11:16–17, 26–29; 19:20–24;
24:2; 27:15–23; Judges 3:9–10; 6:34; 11:29; 2 Kings 2:9–10,15; Ezek.
1:28; 2:8; 3:22–27; 1 Sam. 10:5–13; 19:24; 2 Sam. 23:1–2.
[17] See Ps. 52:12–19; 143:4, 7, 10; Isa. 30:1; 32:15–17; 57:15; 63:10;
Wis. 9:17.

the Messiah will be possessed without limits by
the Spirit of God, and also because at the time of
the Messiah there will be an intense outpouring
of the Spirit of Yahweh.[18]

New Testament

This is where the full revelation of the Holy Spirit as the third Person
of the Holy Trinity appears. The Spirit of God fills John the Baptist
before being born, it takes Mary to the dynamism of the Most High,
it is transmitted to Elizabeth, it is transmitted to Zechariah, and
ends up resting on Simeon.[19]

Jesus has the Spirit of God upon Him, He is "moved" by Him,
drawn by His dynamism, with the fullness conferred by His dual
quality as Messiah and Son. He begins His ministry "filled with the
Holy Spirit," which He possesses as Son. He will send it to His apostles
after His Ascension and will communicate to them the dynamism
and ardor necessary to carry His witness to the ends of the earth.[20]

It was realized on the day of Pentecost with wind and fire, according to the prophecy of Joel, the announcement of the Baptist,
and the promise of Jesus. This first outpouring was then renewed
collectively on various occasions, either by divine initiative, at the
request of the apostles, as a direct gift from God and more precisely
from Jesus, or through the rite of the laying on of hands.[21]

The Spirit thus received is a prophetic Spirit, the one who spoke
through the prophets; it is also a Spirit of faith and wisdom or

---

[18] See Isa. 11:1ff; 32:1ff; 42:1ff; 44:2–3; Ezek. 11:14ff; 36:26–27; Zech. 12:10; 13:1–5.
[19] See Luke 1:15–17; 1:35, 41, 45, 67; 2:25–27; Mt 1:18–20.
[20] See Matt. 3:16; John 1:32–33; 16:7; Luke 4:1; 10:21; 4:14, 16, 21; Mark 3:11; Acts 1:4–8.
[21] See Acts 2:1, 4; 2:23, 33; 4:31; 8:14–19; 10:44–45; 11:6–16; 15:8; 19:2–6.

dynamism, like that of Christ. It makes one speak in all tongues and gives the power to forgive sins. It descends in a permanent way on all the disciples of Jesus, as on Jesus Himself; it constantly directs the apostles and their collaborators as Master, but it can also be resisted.[22]

In His wonderful sermon at the Last Supper, Jesus tells His disciples that the Holy Spirit will teach them all things, and that He will bring to their remembrance all that He has said, will guide them to the complete truth, and will communicate to them the things to come. He will glorify Christ, because He will take from Him and make Him known to the apostles.[23]

St. Paul wonderfully specifies the theology of the Holy Spirit. He is the Spirit of God and of Christ; His operation is the same as that of the Father and of the Son and makes the just temples of God and of the Holy Spirit Himself. For the faithful, He is the beginning of life in Christ, although it is true that to live in Christ and to live in the Spirit are one and the same thing. He is the distributor of every gift; He searches God's secrets; He is the gift par excellence; He moves us in such a way that we please God and must never sadden Him.[24]

Finally, the formula of Baptism, dictated by Christ Himself, places the Holy Spirit on a plane of equality with the Father and the Son; and in the letters of St. Paul the three Divine Persons are constantly associated. Thus the Spirit of God, who hovered over the primitive chaos at the dawn of Creation, appears later as a personal being who manifests Himself in the promotion of faithful souls and of Christian society, and who makes us invoke with unspeakable

[22] See Acts 1:8, 16; 2:4–18; 4:31; 6:3, 5; 7:51; 10:38–46; 11:24; John 1:2; 5:3–9; 6:3–5; 8:29; 10:19; 17:51; 20:21–23.
[23] See John 14:26; 16:13–14.
[24] See Rom. 1:4; 5:5; 8:1–27; 1 Cor. 2:10–14; 3:16; 6:11, 19; 12:3–13; 2 Cor. 3:17; Tit. 3:4–7; Gal. 4:6; 6:7–8; Eph. 4:1–6, 30.

groans the revelation of the children of God and the redemption of our bodies. He will be the one who will bring about the definitive coming of Christ.[25]

These are the fundamental data that Sacred Scripture gives us about the Person of the Holy Spirit. On the basis of these and of those facts supplied by Tradition (itself a legitimate source of divine revelation alongside the Bible, under the proper conditions), theologians have constructed the complete theology of the Holy Spirit in the form that we will see in the following pages.

[25] See Matt. 28:19; Gal. 4:6; Rom. 8:14–17, 26; 15:25–16; 1 Cor. 12:4–6; 2 Cor. 1:21–22; 13:13; Tit. 3.4–6; Heb. 9:14; Rev. 22:17.

CHAPTER 3

Different Names of the Holy Spirit

IN ORDER TO know a little less imperfectly the intimate nature, proper or appropriate, of any of the Divine Persons in particular, it is very useful and profitable to examine the different names by which Sacred Scripture, Tradition, and the liturgy of the Church call that particular Person, for each of them contains a new aspect or nuance that allows us to know Him a little better. To understand this in its proper limits, it is necessary to explain the difference that exists between the operations proper to each of the Divine Persons and those which, although they are really common to all three, are appropriated to a certain Person because they fit very well with the properties that are peculiar and exclusive to Him. The distinguished abbot of Maredsous writes admirably on this subject:

> As you know, in God there is only one intelligence, only one will, only one power, because there is only one divine nature; but there is also a distinction of Persons. Such a distinction results from the mysterious operations that take place there in the intimate life of God and from the mutual relations that derive from these operations. The Father begets the Son, and the Holy Spirit proceeds from both. To beget, to be

Father, is the personal and exclusive property of the first Person; to be Son is the personal and exclusive property of the second; and to proceed from the Father and the Son by way of love is the personal and exclusive property of the Holy Spirit.

These personal properties establish between the Father, the Son, and the Holy Spirit mutual relations, whence the distinction. But apart from these personal properties and relations, everything is common and indivisible among the Divine Persons—intelligence, will, power, and majesty—because the same indivisible divine nature is common to the three Persons. Here is what little we can trace about the intimate operations of God.

As for the external works—that is, the actions that are completed outside of God (operations ad extra), whether in the material world, as in the action of directing every creature to its end, or in the world of souls, as in the action of producing grace—they are common to the three Divine Persons. Why is this so? Because the source of these operations ad extra, of these works exterior to the intimate life of God, is the divine nature, and that nature is one and indivisible for the three Persons. The Blessed Trinity works in the world as a single cause.

But God wants men to know and honor not only the divine unity, but also the Trinity of Persons. That is why the Church, for example, in the liturgy, attributes to such a Divine Person certain actions that take place in the world and which, although they are common to the three Divine Persons, have a special relationship or intimate affinity with the place, if I may so express myself, which that Person occupies in the Blessed Trinity—that is, with the properties that are peculiar and exclusive to Him.

Since, therefore, the Father is the source, origin, and principle of the other two Persons, without this implying hierarchical superiority or priority of time in the Father, the works that are verified in the world and that particularly manifest the power, or in which the idea of origin is revealed above all, are attributed to the Father; as, for example, Creation, by which God brought the world out of nothing. In the Creed we say: "I believe in God the Father almighty, creator of Heaven and earth." Could it be, perhaps, that the Father had a greater part in, manifested more of His power in this work than the Son and the Holy Spirit? It would be wrong to think so. The Son and the Holy Spirit acted in the creation of the world as much as the Father, because, as we have said, in their operations toward the outside (ad extra) God worked by His omnipotence, and omnipotence is common to the three Divine Persons. How, then, does the Church speak in this way? Because, in the Blessed Trinity, the Father is the first Person, the beginning without beginning, from which the other two proceed. This is His exclusive personal property, which distinguishes Him from the Son and the Holy Spirit. Precisely so that we do not forget this property, the exterior works are attributed to the Father, which suggest it to us because they have some relation to it.

The same must be said of the Person of the Son, who is the Word in the Trinity, who proceeds from the Father by way of intelligence, by intellectual generation, who is the infinite expression of divine thought, who is considered above all as eternal Wisdom. That is why the works are attributed to Him in whose realization wisdom shines forth above all.

Likewise, with regard to the Holy Spirit, what does He become in the Trinity? He is the ultimate end of the divine operations, of the life of God in Himself. He closes, so to speak, the cycle of this divine intimacy; He is perfection in love and has, as a personal property, the proceeding at the same time from the Father and the Son by way of love. Hence, everything that implies perfection, love, union, and therefore holiness, because our holiness is measured by the greater or lesser degree of our union with God, everything is attributed to the Holy Spirit. But is He, perchance, more sanctifying than the Father and the Son? No, the work of our sanctification is common to the three Divine Persons. But let us repeat that, since the work of holiness in the soul is a work of perfection and union, it is attributed to the Holy Spirit, because in this way we more easily remember His personal properties, in order to honor and adore Him in how He differs from the Father and the Son.

God wants us to take, so to speak, as much to heart the honoring of His Trinity of Persons as His unity of nature. That is why He wants the Church to remind her children, not only that there is only one God, but that this one God is triune in Persons.

This is what in theology we call appropriation. It is inspired by divine revelation, and the Church uses it continually. Its purpose is to highlight the attributes proper to each Divine Person. By bringing out these properties, it also makes us know and love them more and more.[26]

---

[26] Columba Marmion, *Jesus Christ, life of the soul*, I, 6, 1.

Let us now see which names belong to the Holy Spirit in a proper and perfect way, and which others only by a very reasonable appropriation.

Proper Names of the Third Divine Person

According to St. Thomas Aquinas, the three most proper and representative names of the third Divine Person are Holy Spirit, Love, and Gift.[27] Let us examine them one by one.

Holy Spirit. If the two words which compose this name are considered separately, they are equally suitable to the three Divine Persons; all three are Spirit and all three are holy. If they are taken as a single name or denomination, they suit exclusively the third Divine Person, since He alone proceeds from the other two by a common spiration of infinitely holy love.[28]

Catholic doctrine teaches us about this most holy name:

1. That the Holy Spirit proceeds from the Father and the Son: *qui ex Patre Filioque procedit.* This is expressly defined by the Church (Dz 691) against the Eastern Orthodox, who reject the Filioque and affirm that the Holy Spirit proceeds only from the Father.

2. Catholic doctrine is clear. If, by an impossibility, the Holy Spirit did not also proceed from the Son, it would be impossible for the Spirit to be in any way distinguished from the Son. For the Divine Persons cannot be distinguished by something absolute, since then the

---

[27] See STh I, q. 36–38.
[28] Ibid., q. 36 a. 1, c ad 1.

divine essence would not be the same in all of them, but by something relative and opposed to each other — that is, by a relation of origin, which is, properly speaking, what constitutes the Divine Persons as distinct from each other.[29]

3. The Holy Spirit does not proceed from the Father through the Son in the sense that the Son is the final, formal, motivating, or instrumental cause of the exhalation of the Holy Spirit in the Father, but insofar as it means that the exhalative virtue of the Son is communicated to Him by the Father.[30]

4. The Father and the Son constitute a single principle of the Holy Spirit, with a unique spiration common to both.[31]

5. The Holy Spirit is not made, nor created, nor begotten, but proceeds from the Father and the Son (Dz 39).

Love. The word love, referring to God, can be taken in three senses:

1. Essentially, and in this sense it is common to the three Divine Persons.

2. Notionally, and in this way it suits only the Father and the Son: it is their active love, which gives rise to the Holy Spirit.

[29] Ibid., a. 2; *De potentia*, q. 10 a. 5 ad 4; *Contra gentes*, IV, 24.
[30] Ibid., q. 36, a. 3.
[31] Ibid., a. 4.

3. Personally, and in this way it is exclusively suited to the Holy Spirit, as the passive term of the love of the Father and the Son.[32]

It can be affirmed that the Father and the Son love each other in the Holy Spirit, understanding this formula of their notional or originating love, because in this sense to love is nothing other than to breathe out love, as to speak is to produce the verb, and to bloom is to produce flowers.[33]

Gift. The Holy Fathers and the liturgy of the Church (*Veni, Creator*) frequently use the word *gift* to designate the Holy Spirit, which has its foundation in Sacred Scripture (see John 4:10; 7:39; Acts 2:38; 8:20).

The same distinction must be made here as in the previous name, and so:

1. In the essential sense it means everything that can be graciously given by God to rational creatures, whether of the natural or supernatural order. In this sense it applies equally to the three Divine Persons and to the divine essence itself, inasmuch as, through grace, the rational creature can delight in and enjoy God.[34]

2. In the notional or originating sense, it means the Divine Person who, having His origin in another, is given or can be given by Him to the rational creature. In this sense, the name gift can only be

---

[32]   Ibid., q. 37 a. 1.
[33]   Ibid., a. 2.
[34]   Ibid., I, q. 43 a. 2–3.

appropriate to the Son and the Holy Spirit, not to the Father, who cannot be given by anyone, since He proceeds from no one.

3. In the personal sense, it is the same Divine Person to whom it is proper, by virtue of His own origin, to be the proximate reason for every divine gift and for the fact that He Himself is given in a completely gratuitous way to the rational creature, and in this personal sense, the name gift corresponds exclusively to the Holy Spirit, who, because He proceeds by way of love, has the reason of being the first gift, because love is the first thing that we give to a person whenever we grant him any grace.[35]

Names Appropriate to the Holy Spirit

Tradition, the liturgy of the Church, and Sacred Scripture itself have given the Holy Spirit many names. He is called the Paraclete Spirit, Creator Spirit, Spirit of Christ, Comforting Spirit, Spirit of Truth, Virtue of the Most High, Advocate, Finger of God, Guest of the Soul, Seal, Union, Link, Bond, Kiss, Living Fountain, Fire, Spiritual Anointing, Most Beatific Light, Father of the Poor, Giver of Gifts, Light of Hearts, and so on.

Let us briefly examine the foundations of these names appropriate to the Holy Spirit.

1. Paraclete Spirit. Jesus Christ Himself uses this expression alluding to the Holy Spirit (see John 14:16, 26; 15:26; 16:7). Some translate it by the

[35] Ibid., q.38 a.1–2.

word *Teacher*, because Christ Himself says a little later that "he will teach you all things" (John 14:26). Others translate by Comforter, because He will prevent the apostles from feeling orphaned by the gentleness of His consolation (see John 14:18). Others translate the word Paraclete by *Advocate*, who will plead for us, in the words of St. Paul, "with sighs too deep for words" (Rom. 8:26).

2. Creator Spirit. "The Holy Spirit," says St. Thomas, "is the principle of creation."[36] The reason is that God creates things out of love, and love in God is the Holy Spirit. That is why the psalm says: "When thou sendest forth thy Spirit, they are created" (Ps. 103:30).

3. Spirit of Christ. The Holy Spirit completely filled the most holy soul of Christ (see Luke 4:1). In the synagogue of Nazareth, Christ applied to Himself the following text from Isaiah: "The Spirit of the Lord God is upon me" (Isa. 61:1; see Luke 4:18). St. Paul says that "any one who does not have the Spirit of Christ does not belong to him" (Rom. 8:9); but "if the Spirit of him who raised Jesus from the dead dwells in you, he who raised Christ Jesus from the dead will give life to your mortal bodies also through his Spirit who dwells in you" (Rom. 8:11).

4. Spirit of Truth. This is an expression Christ Himself applied to the Holy Spirit: "The Spirit

---

[36] *Contra gentes*, IV, 20. St. Thomas' commentary on this and the following two chapters is admirable.

of truth, whom the world cannot receive, because it neither sees him nor knows him" (John
14:17). According to St. Cyril and St. Augustine,
it means the true Spirit of God, and is opposed
to the spirit of the world, to deceitful and falla-
cious wisdom. That is why the Savior adds
"which the world cannot receive," because "the
unspiritual man does not receive the gifts of the
Spirit of God, for they are folly to him, and he is
not able to understand them because they are
spiritually discerned" (1 Cor. 2:14).

5. Virtue of the Most High. This is the expression
used by the angel at the Annunciation when He
explains to Mary how the mystery of the Incarnation will be accomplished: "The Holy Spirit
will come upon you, and the power of the Most
High will overshadow you" (Luke 1:35). Other
Gospel passages also allude to the "power from
on high" (see Luke 24:49).

6. Finger of God. In the hymn *Veni, Creator Spiritus*, the Church designates the Holy Spirit with
this mysterious expression: "Finger of the right
hand of the Father," Digitus paternae dexterae. It
is a metaphor very rich in content and very fruitful in applications. Because in the fingers of the
hand, especially the right hand, is all our con-
structive and creative power. That is why Scripture places the power of God in His hands: the
tablets of the Old Law were written by the "finger of God" (Deut. 9:10); the heavens are "the
work of thy fingers" (Ps. 8:3); the magicians of
Pharaoh had to recognize that in the wonders of

Moses there was "the finger of God" (Exod. 8:15), and Christ cast out demons "by the finger of God" (Luke 11:20). This expression, applied to the Holy Spirit, is therefore very appropriate to signify that through Him all the wonders of God are accomplished, especially in the order of grace and sanctification.

7. Guest of the Soul. In the sequence of Pentecost, the Holy Spirit is called "sweet guest of the soul": *dulcis hospes animae.* The indwelling of God in the soul of the just corresponds equally to the three Divine Persons of the Blessed Trinity, since it is an operation ad extra (see John 14:23; 1 Cor 3:16–17); but since it is a work of love, and these are attributed in a special way to the Holy Spirit, He is considered in a very special way as the most sweet guest of our souls (see 1 Cor 6:19).

8. Seal. St. Paul says that we have been "sealed with the promised Holy Spirit" (Eph. 1:13), and also that "it is God who establishes us with you in Christ, and has commissioned us; he has put his seal upon us and given us his Spirit in our hearts as a guarantee" (2 Cor. 1:21–22).

9. Union, Nexus, Bond, Kiss. These are names that express the inseparable and very close union between the Father and the Son by virtue of the Holy Spirit, who proceeds from both by a common spiration of love.

10. Living Fountain, Fire, Charity, Spiritual Anointing. Expressions of the hymn *Veni, Creator,*

which fit very well with the character and personality of the Holy Spirit.

11. Most Blessed Light, Father of the Poor, Giver of
Gifts, Light of Hearts. All these expressions are
applied by the Church to the Holy Spirit in the
magnificent sequence of Pentecost, *Veni, Sancte
Spiritus*.

These are the principal names that Sacred Scripture, Tradition, and
the liturgy of the Church appropriate to the Holy Spirit because
of the great affinity or similarity that exists between them and the
characteristics proper to the third Person of the Blessed Trinity. All
of them, well meditated, contain great practical teachings to intensify in our souls the love and veneration of the sanctifying Spirit, to
whose perfect docility and obedience is linked the progressive and
ascending march toward the highest sanctity.

CHAPTER 4

The Holy Spirit in Jesus Christ

AFTER HAVING BRIEFLY studied the Person of the Holy Spirit in the bosom of the Most Blessed Trinity, through the data of Sacred Scripture and the different names by which Scripture, Tradition, and the liturgy of the Church call Him, we will now examine His principal operations in the Person of Jesus Christ, in the Church, and in the interior of faithful souls.

Let us begin with our Lord Jesus Christ, true God and true man. Let us approach with respect the Divine Person of the incarnate Word in order to contemplate something of the marvels that the Holy Spirit worked in Him at the moment of His Incarnation and throughout His life.[37]

The main episodes in the life of Jesus in which the Holy Spirit was most especially present are the following: Incarnation, sanctification, Baptism in the Jordan, temptations in the desert, Transfiguration, miracles, evangelical doctrine, and in all His human activities. Let us go through them one by one.

Incarnation

The masterpiece of the Holy Spirit is undoubtedly His decisive participation in the ineffable mystery of the Incarnation of the Word in

---

[37]   A. Arrighini, *Il Dio ignoto*, 153ff.; Columba Marmion, *Jesus Christ, life of the soul*, w.c., I, 6, 1.

the virgin womb of Mary. In reality, the Incarnation of the Word is a divine operation ad extra and, therefore, common to the three Divine Persons. The three Divine Persons concurred together in this ineffable work, although it must be added immediately that it had as its final end only the Word: the Word alone, the Son of God, was the only one who became incarnate or became man.[38] Although it is a work accomplished in unison by the three Divine Persons, it is attributed in a special way to the Holy Spirit, and this by a very convenient and reasonable appropriation. For since the Incarnation of the Word is the greatest proof of love that God has given to His rational creatures, to the point that it filled Christ Himself with admiration — "God so loved the world that he gave his only Son" (John 3:16) — what is so strange about attributing it in a very special way to the Holy Spirit, who is personally the substantial Love, the infinite Love in the bosom of the Most Blessed Trinity? Tradition has always recognized and proclaimed this since apostolic times, and for this reason it has always repeated in the Symbol of Faith: "I believe in Jesus Christ our Lord, who was conceived by the power and grace of the Holy Spirit and was born of the Virgin Mary." The Creed does no more than repeat the words addressed to Mary by the angel at the Annunciation: "The Holy Spirit will rest upon you, and the power of the Most High will overshadow you, and for this reason the child you have begotten will be holy, and will be called the Son of God" (Luke 1:35).

In this way, the third Person of the Blessed Trinity becomes wonderfully fruitful, no less than the other two. In fact, while the fruitfulness of the Father appears clearly in the eternal generation of the

---

[38] To use an image used by some Fathers of the Church, we will say that when a person puts on his own clothes and is helped by two others, the three of them concur in the same work, even if only one of them comes out dressed. Of course, this image, like any other that could be used, is very imperfect and fails in many aspects.

Son, and that of the Son in the procession of the Holy Spirit together with the Father, the Holy Spirit remained apparently sterile, since it is impossible to produce a fourth Person in the Trinity. Now then, by the Virgin Mary consenting with her fiat to the Incarnation of the Word through the work of the Holy Spirit, she mystically becomes the spouse of the same divine Spirit and makes Him divinely fecund in a most pure and most holy, but no less real and true, way. It is certain and evident that the Holy Spirit did not create the divinity of the Word, but only the humanity of Jesus in order to unite it hypostatically to the Word; nor did He create the humanity of His own divine substance, which would be monstrous and absurd, but by using His divine power on the blood and virginal flesh of the Immaculate Mother of God. St. Ambrose expressed the great mystery in these simple and brief words: "In what way did Mary conceive of the Holy Spirit? If it was of her own divine substance, one would have to say that the Spirit became flesh and bones. But it was not so, but only by His operation and power."[39] Thus, continues the holy Doctor, from the immaculate flesh of a living virgin, the Holy Spirit formed the Second Adam, just as from a virgin earth the Creator God formed the first.

Sanctification

As Catholic theology teaches and as is the official doctrine of the Church, in addition to the grace called union or hypostatic grace, by virtue of which Christ as man is personally the Son of God, His most holy soul possesses with immense fullness habitual or sanctifying grace, whose effusion in the soul of Christ is also attributed to the Holy Spirit.[40]

---

[39] St. Ambrose, *De Spiritu Sancto*, II, 5.

[40] We have extensively studied everything related to the grace of Christ–of union, sanctifying and capital–in another of our works published by Biblioteca de Autores Cristianos: A. Royo Marín, *Jesucristo y la vida cristiana* (Madrid: BAC, 1961) 73–98.

To understand this doctrine, we must keep in mind that in Jesus there are two distinct natures, both perfect, but united in the Person who links them: the Word. The grace of union makes the human nature subsist in the Divine Person of the Word. This grace is entirely unique, transcendent, and incommunicable: only Christ possesses it. By it belongs to the Word the humanity of Christ, which becomes, by the same token, the humanity of the true Son of God, and which is, therefore, the object of infinite pleasure for the Eternal Father. But even when the human nature is so intimately united to the Word, it is not thereby annihilated or rendered inactive; on the contrary, it retains and preserves its essence, its integrity, with all its energies and powers; it is capable of action, and it is sanctifying grace that elevates this holy humanity so that it can act supernaturally.

Developing this same idea in other terms, it can be said that the grace of union or hypostatic grace unites human nature to the Person of the Word, and thus divinizes the very essence of Christ: Christ is, through it, a divine "subject." So much for the purpose of this grace of union, proper and exclusive to Jesus Christ. But this human nature must also be beautified by sanctifying grace so that it can work in a supernatural or divine way in each of its faculties. This sanctifying grace, which is connatural to the grace of union — that is, which in a certain sense flows from the grace of union in a natural way — brings the soul of Christ to the height of His union with the Word; it allows the human nature, which subsists in the Word by virtue of the grace of union, to act as befits a soul sublimated to such an exalted dignity and produce divine fruits.

This is why sanctifying grace was not given to the soul of Christ, as to the elect, but in the highest degree, with an immense fullness. Now the effusion of sanctifying grace in the soul of Christ is attributed to the Holy Spirit. Christ applied to Himself in the synagogue of Nazareth the following messianic text from Isaiah: "The Spirit of the Lord God is upon me, because the Lord has anointed me to bring good tidings to the afflicted" (Isa. 61:1; Luke 4:18). Our Lord made His own the words of Isaiah, who compares the action of the Holy Spirit to an anointing.[41] The grace of the Holy Spirit spread over Jesus like the oil of joy that first consecrated Him as the Son of God and Messiah, and then, at the very moment of His Incarnation, filled Him with the fullness of His gifts and the abundance of divine treasures.

For we must not forget that sanctifying grace is never infused alone. It is always accompanied by the very rich combination of the infused virtues and the gifts of the Holy Spirit. Grace itself informs the essence of the soul, divinizing it and elevating it to the supernatural order; just as the virtues and gifts inform the various powers in order to elevate them to the same plane and make them capable of producing supernatural or divine acts.

This is why the prophet Isaiah, speaking of the future Messiah, announces the fullness of the gifts with which His most holy soul will be enriched: "There shall come forth a shoot from the stump of Jesse, and a branch shall grow out of his roots. And the Spirit of the Lord shall rest upon him, the spirit of wisdom and understanding, the spirit of counsel and might, the spirit of knowledge and the fear of the Lord. And his delight shall be in the fear of the Lord" (Isa. 11:1–3). Tradition has always seen in this text the fullness of the gifts of the Holy Spirit in the most holy soul of Christ.

In no one have such gifts ever produced such sublime fruits of holiness. Even as a man, Jesus presents Himself with a perfection that infinitely surpasses that of anyone else; no matter how holy

---

[41] In the Catholic liturgy (*Veni, Creator Spiritus*) the Holy Spirit is called "spiritual anointing" (*spiritalis unctio*).

he may be, St. Paul considers himself the least of the apostles and unworthy to be called an apostle (1 Cor. 15:9). St. John affirms that if anyone considers himself sinless, he deceives himself and the truth is not in him (1 John 1:8). "I do not know," writes De Maistre, "what the heart of an evildoer is; I know no more than that of an honest man, and it is dreadful."[42] All upright consciences have always expressed themselves in a similar way. Not so in Jesus Christ. In Him, there is no repentance, no desire for a better life. He challenged His enemies: "Which of you convicts me of sin?" (John 8:46), and neither the Scribes and Pharisees, nor Pilate, nor Herod, nor any of His great enemies have ever been able to catch Him in the least sin. The holiness of Jesus has always triumphed: He is "holy, blameless, unstained, separated from sinners, exalted above the heavens" (Heb. 7:26), adorned with all the gifts and replete with all the fruits of the Holy Spirit. All the virtues flourished in Him with the same exuberant and gigantic vegetation: no void, not even the slightest mole. He is perfect holiness, the very holiness of God.

Baptism

The treasures of holiness and grace that we have just recalled were poured out by the Holy Spirit into the soul of Christ at the very moment of the Incarnation of the Word in the virgin womb of Mary, but they were realized in a quiet way hidden from the eyes of the world. It was fitting, therefore, that later His infinite holiness should be publicly manifested and His divinity proclaimed by the Eternal Father Himself in the presence of the Holy Spirit, and this is precisely what happened at the Baptism of Jesus by John the Baptist.[43]

---

[42] J. de Maistre, *Las veladas de san Petersburgo*, (Valencia: Imprenta de J. Gimeno, 1832).

[43] See STh III, q. 39 a. 8 ad 3.

The evangelical scene is well known:

> Then Jesus came from Galilee to the Jordan to John, to
> be baptized by him. John would have prevented him,
> saying, "I need to be baptized by you, and do you come
> to me?" But Jesus answered him, "Let it be so now; for
> thus it is fitting for us to fulfil all righteousness." Then
> he consented. And when Jesus was baptized, he went
> up immediately from the water, and behold, the heav-
> ens were opened and he saw the Spirit of God descend-
> ing like a dove, and alighting on him; and lo, a voice
> from heaven, saying, "This is my beloved Son, with
> whom I am well pleased" (Matt. 3:13–17).

The Angelic Doctor, St. Thomas Aquinas, beautifully notes that, at
the moment of His Baptism, it was most convenient that the Holy
Spirit descended upon Jesus in the form of a dove, to signify that
everyone who receives Christ's Baptism becomes a temple and tabernacle of the Holy Spirit and must lead a life full of simplicity and
candor, like that of the dove, as Christ Himself warns in the Gospel
(Matt. 10:16).[44] It was also most convenient that in Christ's Baptism
the voice of the Father should be heard proclaiming His pleasure
in Him, because Christian Baptism, of which John the Baptist's
was a figure, is consecrated by the invocation and the virtue of the
Holiest Trinity, and in the Baptism of Christ the whole trinitarian
mystery was made manifest: the voice of the Father, the presence of
the Son, and the descent of the Holy Spirit in the form of a dove.[45]
Finally, it should be noted that the Father manifested Himself very
opportunely in the voice, because it is proper to the Father to beget

[44] Ibid., a. 6 c and ad 4.
[45] Ibid., q. 39 a. 8.

the word, which means the Word. Hence the very voice emitted by the Father bears witness to the filiation of the Word.[46]

Temptations in the Desert

The three synoptic evangelists relate the mysterious scene of the temptations that Jesus suffered in the desert by the devil, and all three tell us that He was led or pushed into the desert by the Holy Spirit Himself. Here are their own words:

> "Then Jesus was led up by the Spirit into the wilderness to be tempted by the devil" (Matt. 4:1).

> "The Spirit immediately drove him out into the wilderness. And he was in the wilderness forty days, tempted by Satan" (Mark 1:12–13).

> "And Jesus, full of the Holy Spirit, returned from the Jordan, and was led by the Spirit for forty days in the wilderness, tempted by the devil" (Luke 4:1–2).

The fact that He was driven by the Holy Spirit Himself into the wilderness to be tempted by the devil raises a number of theological difficulties that must be explained if we are to understand this mysterious passage.

In the first place, it is worth asking why the Holy Spirit led or pushed Jesus into the desert: did the Son of God need to submit to penance, fasting, or, what is even stranger, to the temptations of the devil?

It is evident that He did not. St. Paul tells us that since Jesus was "holy, blameless, unstained, separated from sinners, exalted above the

---

[46] Ibid., ad. 2.

heavens, He has no need, like those high priests, to offer sacrifices daily, first for his own sins and then for those of the people; he did this once for all when he offered up himself" (Heb. 7:26). St. Paul himself gives us the true explanation when he tells us that Christ was tempted to help us overcome temptations (Heb 2:18) and to sympathize with our weaknesses, being tempted in all things like as we are (Heb 4:15).

To give us an effective example of mortification, during the forty days that He remained in the desert He ate absolutely nothing (Luke 4:2). Abandoning Himself to the impulse of the Holy Spirit, who transported Him to that accursed desert, He completely segregated Himself from the outside world. Not even feeling that He had a body that needed to be nourished and preserved from the ravages of the climate and the wild beasts, He gave Himself entirely to prayer and to the grave thoughts that filled His spirit as He was about to begin His public mission to the chosen people. On the other hand, recent discoveries have shown that, even without supernatural help, man can live six or seven weeks, or even somewhat longer, without receiving any food. Such a situation, however, must necessarily come to an end, and then the violated nature claims its rights with a special energy — that is why St. Luke expressly says that, at the end of forty days, Jesus "was hungry" (Luke 4:2). This was the moment that the devil chose to give a more precise and violent form to the temptations with which, perhaps since the first days of the retreat, He had been besieging Jesus. From the Gospel itself, in fact, it seems to follow that these temptations followed one after another throughout the time Jesus spent in the desert (see Mark 1:13). The three that the evangelists refer to in particular, and which are known to all, gathered at the end of the forty days, would be a summary or a rehearsal of the others.

In connection with these mysterious temptations, it is also worth asking to what extent they could have influenced the soul of Christ and to what extent the Holy Spirit would have abandoned Him to the mercy of the spirit of evil, and that this would have offended Him.

In order to resolve this question correctly, it is necessary to keep in mind that there are three principles from which the temptations that men suffer proceed: the world, the devil, and the flesh or sensuality itself, which are, by the same token, the three principal enemies of the soul.

Now, Christ could not suffer the assaults of the third of these enemies, since neither the fomes peccati nor the slightest inclination to sin existed in Him (see Dz 224). Nor could the pomps and vanities of the world affect Him at all, given His clairvoyance and serenity of judgment. But there is no inconvenience in His voluntarily submitting Himself to diabolical suggestion, since it is something purely external to the one who suffers it and does not suppose the slightest imperfection in Him. All the malice of this temptation belongs exclusively to the tempter.[47]

In any case, the theological explanation of this question involves great difficulty, since it is intimately related to the mystery of the hypostatic union and to that of the essential union of the three Divine Persons among themselves. It is evident, in fact, that if we suppose the soul of Christ to be always equal and necessarily illuminated by the direct communication of the Word and by the effusion of the Holy Spirit, the temptation could be for Him neither dangerous nor meritorious; it would not be a struggle, but a mere appearance of struggle, a useless and deceptive phantasmagoria. If the divine irradiation endures always in the same way and with the same intensity in the depths of the Savior's consciousness, the manifestations of joy or sadness so profoundly expressed in the Gospel will have no meaning, not excluding that last and supreme cry of anguish: "My God, my God, why hast thou forsaken me?" (Matt. 27:46)

---

[47] Ibid., q. 41 a. 1 ad 3.

How can all this be explained? Theologians of all schools agree in saying that, in the hours of trial, the Divinity withdrew, so to speak, to the upper part of the soul of Christ and covered itself as with a veil; that is to say, that the Word and the other two Divine Persons suspended their luminous communication and left the human soul of Christ as if at the mercy of itself. Just as a mother seems to leave her little child to experience for himself his own strength when he takes his first steps, apparently withdrawing the protection of her maternal hands but remaining vigilant and alert so that the child does not fall to the ground if, unfortunately, he stumbles when starting to walk or when struggling against an obstacle, it is evident that the fact of not falling over the obstacle constitutes for the child a victory and a merit, regardless of whether he had the protection of the maternal arms assured if he had need of them. In the temptations of Jesus, the presence of the Word and of the other two Persons of the Trinity always assured the most resounding and absolute triumph; but this notwithstanding, the momentary isolation in which they left His human soul established a true merit and an indisputable triumph for it. In those moments of trial, Jesus seemed to have lost His powers as God, to retain only the weakness of the slave; but His most holy humanity was so pure and so well guarded by the Divinity, that it was absolutely impeccable.

Of course, here are the main reasons why Christ wanted to submit to Satan's temptations:

1. So that we may deserve help against temptations.

2. So that no one, no matter how holy he may be, may consider himself safe and exempt from temptation.

3. To teach us how to overcome them.

4. To give us confidence in His mercy, according to
the words of St. Paul: "Our high priest is not
such as cannot sympathize with our weaknesses,
but was in all points tempted like as we are,
without sin" (Heb 4:15).[48]

The Transfiguration on Tabor

The Synoptic Gospels describe in detail the dazzling scene of Christ's
Transfiguration on a "high mountain," which was probably Tabor.
Christ's face became radiant like the sun, and His clothes became white
as light, in the presence of Peter, James, and John; moments later a shining cloud covered them, and a voice came out of it saying: "This is my
beloved Son, with whom I am well pleased; listen to him" (Matt. 17:1–9).

Why did Jesus want to be transfigured in this way in the presence
of His three favorite disciples? The immediate historical reason was
undoubtedly to raise the spirits of those disciples to whom He had
just announced His coming Passion and death (see Matt. 16:21). He
had also just told them: "If any man would come after me, let him
deny himself and take up his cross and follow me" (Matt. 16:24).
Faced with such a hard prospect, it is quite natural that the disciples
experienced a certain dejection and sadness. To lift their spirits, Christ
showed them, in the scene of the Transfiguration, the immense glory
that awaited them if they remained faithful to Him until death.[49]

But what we are interested in emphasizing here is the presence
of the entire Blessed Trinity in the scene of Tabor. The voice of the
Father is heard, as in the Baptism of Jesus, in the presence of His
beloved Son and of the Holy Spirit, symbolized in the resplendent
cloud. Let us listen to the Angelic Doctor expounding this doctrine:

[48] See ibid., a. 1.
[49] See STh III, q. 45 a. 1.

Just as at the Baptism of Jesus, in which the mystery of the first regeneration was declared, the operation of the whole Trinity was manifested, for there the incarnate Son was present, the Holy Spirit appeared in the form of a dove, and the Father was manifested in the voice, so also, at the Transfiguration, in which the mystery of the future glorification was announced, the whole Trinity appeared: the Father in the voice, the Son in the man, and the Holy Spirit in the shining cloud. For as in Baptism God confers innocence, designated by the simplicity of the dove, so in the resurrection He will give to His elect the brightness of glory and refreshment from all evil, designated by the luminous cloud.[50]

The Miracles

As we saw above, in the synagogue in Nazareth, Jesus applied to Himself the following messianic text from Isaiah:

> The Spirit of the Lord is upon me, because he has anointed me to preach good news to the poor. He has sent me to proclaim release to the captives and recovering of sight to the blind, to set at liberty those who are oppressed, to proclaim the acceptable year of the Lord (Luke 4:18–19).

The Holy Spirit was indeed upon Jesus Christ when He worked His great wonders and miracles, as is clear from the way He performed them.

He carried them out as master and lord of the nature that the Holy Spirit, with His creative breath, had vivified from the

---

[50] Ibid., a. 4 ad 2.

beginning. He performed them without any effort, with the same calm with which He announced the Beatitudes to the people. To perform such wonders, Jesus had no need to beg anyone, to have recourse to the help of Heaven, as happens with the thaumaturgical saints, in whom the gifts of the Holy Spirit are found in a limited and transitory form. A word, even a gesture is enough for Him. He says to the leper: "I will; be clean." Immediately he was cleansed of his leprosy (Matt. 8:2–3). He commands the paralytic: "Rise, take up your pallet, and walk," and He is obeyed at once (John 5:8–9). He cries out to Lazarus: "Lazarus, come out!" and the rotting dead man rises from his tomb full of health and life (see John 11:43–44). It is enough that He stretches out His hand and the storms are calmed, the water becomes wine, the loaves and fish multiply, the demons flee, the angels descend from Paradise.

Let us note still that Jesus does all this no longer for the glory of another, to prove the truth of another's message, to inspire confidence toward Heaven, but for His own glory, to prove the truth of His own religion, to inspire faith and confidence in Himself, in order that He, together with the Father and the Holy Spirit, with whom He is one, may be recognized, loved, and adored. He proclaims Himself, no less than the Father and the Holy Spirit, the source of those miracles, and exclaims: "Truly, truly, I say to you, he who believes in me will also do the works that I do; and greater works than these will he do, because I go to the Father" (John 14:12). And indeed, the apostles and the saints also performed great wonders, perhaps even greater than those of Christ, but always in the name of Christ, by the virtue of Christ, by faith in Jesus Christ, *in fide nominis eius* (Acts 3:16), while Christ Himself performed them by His own virtue, by His own faith, by His own divine power, by the Spirit (John 14:12).

If He baptizes, if He casts out demons from the possessed, if He heals the sick, if He confers the power to forgive sins, it is always in virtue of the Holy Spirit, with whom He forms one in union with the Father. That is why He wants Him to be adored and glorified, to the point of solemnly affirming: "Every sin and blasphemy will be forgiven men, but the blasphemy against the Spirit will not be forgiven. And whoever says a word against the Son of man will be forgiven; but whoever speaks against the Holy Spirit will not be forgiven, either in this age or in the age to come" (Matt. 12:31–32).

Evangelical Doctrine

Also in the sublime doctrine of Christ one feels the Holy Spirit continually fluttering with His gifts of wisdom, understanding, knowledge, and counsel. His words are filled with the divine Spirit in substance as well as form.

In the first place, let us consider its external form. Never have more sublime thoughts, more profound concepts, been expressed with fewer words; and never have words, so heavy and material in themselves, which constitute the despair of writers, been so idealized and vivified in thought. The splendid affirmation of Jesus Christ Himself is not hyperbolic, but the exact expression of the most august reality: "My words are spirit and life" (John 6:63). Science has not yet been able to find the way to enclose in a small volume the immense wealth of human knowledge; but Jesus Christ fully succeeded in enclosing in a few clear, distinct words, radiant with light, the eternal laws of things, the fundamental principles of individuals and peoples, the life and indefinite progress of humanity.

Another impressive characteristic of the doctrine of Christ is its universality. It does not belong to a particular homeland; it is of all nations. It has no age; it is for all times. Christ preached His doctrine in Palestine twenty centuries ago. But still today we do not have to change a single one of His discourses, a single one of His parables, of His maxims, of His sublime teachings, and it is because

His doctrine is nothing other than the genuine expression of the truth, and the truth never changes no matter how much places and times may vary.

The doctrine of the gospel reveals itself to be divine and truly full of the Holy Spirit even in its very substance. Every sentence contains treasures of infinite wisdom, the seeds of ever new and marvelous life. Christ has said, "Blessed are the poor, those who mourn, those who suffer persecution for righteousness' sake." Wonderful seeds! Who can estimate the rich harvest they have produced? From them have come the apostles, the martyrs, the virgins, the best benefactors of humanity. Jesus proclaimed, "Give to God what is God's and to Caesar what is Caesar's," and thus established the fundamental bases of the two powers from which human civilization proceeds. He proclaimed, "All men are brothers," thus outlining the broad lines of social equality. He also said, "Our Father, who art in heaven...," opening the hearts and lips of all to the holiest and most efficacious of prayers. We have rightly said that each of His words contains a seed of indefinite progress. Mankind walks, walks swiftly without ceasing; it blesses and acclaims as it passes the geniuses and heroes who rise up to guide it; but very soon it forgets them and turns its back upon them. Plato's philosophy had great success in former times, but today it is no longer sufficient. Newton's science is admirable, but it has been surpassed. Cuvier's geology raised a revolution, but nobody remembers it anymore. Aristotle, Copernicus, Galileo, Leibniz—all are surpassed. Only Jesus and His doctrine, declares Renan himself, will never be bested.[51] What man, what era, what philosophical system has been able to surpass His thought, or has at least been able to understand it entirely and apply it perfectly to life? Let the world respond with its cry of anguish. Men have

[51] E. Renan, *Life of Jesus* (Barcelona: Maucci, 1903).

divided up the garments of Jesus, they have cast lots for His useless robe; but has the spirit that was so energetically stirred in Him been exhausted, possessed, or entirely understood? By no means. It remains and will always remain inexhaustible, because it is infinite as God, eternal as truth; for it is none other than the Holy Spirit.

The apostles themselves, disciples of the divine Master, did not always succeed in understanding Him, so the Master Himself left to the Holy Spirit the task of completing His teachings: "But the Counselor, the Holy Spirit, whom the Father will send in my name, he will teach you all things, and bring to your remembrance all that I have said to you" (John 14:26). Jesus leaves to the Holy Spirit the task and the glory of completing His doctrine, of deducing the ultimate consequences, of applying it practically — which, as is well known, is always the most difficult part and can only be done conveniently by the one from whom the doctrine comes, and the evangelical doctrine, in fact, proceeded no less from the Word than from the Holy Spirit, being as they are one with the Father.

Human Activities

The Gospels show us how the soul of Jesus Christ, in all its activity, obeyed the inspirations of the Holy Spirit. The Spirit, as we have seen, drives Him into the desert, where He is tempted by the devil (Matt. 4:1). After forty days in the desert, the same Spirit leads Him back to Galilee (Luke 4:14). By the action of this Spirit He casts the demons out of the body of the possessed (Matt. 12:28). Under the action of the Holy Spirit He leaps for joy when He gives thanks to His Father because He reveals divine secrets to simple souls (Luke 10:21).

Finally, St. Paul tells us that Christ's masterpiece, the one in which His love for the Father and His charity for us shines forth, the bloody sacrifice of the Cross for the salvation of the world, was offered by Christ at the prompting of the Holy Spirit, "who through the eternal Spirit offered himself without blemish to God" (Heb. 9:14).

What do all these revelations indicate to us, if not that the Spirit of love guided all the human activity of Christ? Undoubtedly it was Christ Himself, the incarnate Word, who performed His own works; all His actions are the actions of the one Person of the Word, in whom His human nature subsists. Nevertheless, Christ always worked by inspiration and at the impulse of the Holy Spirit. The soul of Jesus, converted into the soul of the Word by the hypostatic union, was also filled with sanctifying grace and worked at all times by the gentle motion of the Holy Spirit.

Hence all the actions of Christ, even those of the most trivial appearance, were absolutely holy. His soul, though created like all other souls, was most holy. In the first place, because it was united to the Word, united to a Divine Person; such a union made of it, from the first moment of the Incarnation, not just any saint, but the Holy One par excellence, the very Son of God. It was holy, moreover, because it was beautified with sanctifying grace in the highest possible degree of perfection, which enabled it to act supernaturally in everything and in perfect consonance with the ineffable union that constitutes its inalienable privilege. It was holy, in the third place, because all its actions and operations, even though they were acts performed solely by the incarnate Word, were carried out under the motion and inspiration of the Holy Spirit, the Spirit of love and holiness. The God-Man is, without a doubt, the masterpiece of the Holy Spirit.

CHAPTER 5

The Holy Spirit in the Church

WE HAVE SEEN in the previous chapter some of the principal marvels that the Holy Spirit worked in the adored Person of our Lord Jesus Christ. The logical order of ideas leads us now to contemplate the action of the Holy Spirit in the Church, founded by Christ Himself, the Savior of the world.

Let us first listen to Dom Columba Marmion's brief but luminous presentation:

> Before ascending to Heaven, Jesus promised His disciples that He would pray to the Father to give them the Holy Spirit, and He made this gift of the Spirit to our souls the object of a special supplication: "I will pray the Father and he will give you another Helper, the Spirit of truth" (John 14:16–17), and you know how Jesus' request was answered, with what abundance the Holy Spirit was given to the apostles on the day of Pentecost. From that day dates, so to speak, the taking possession by the divine Spirit of the Church, the Mystical Body of Christ; and we can add that, if Christ is the Head of the Church, the Holy Spirit is the soul of that Body. It is He who guides and inspires the Church, keeping her, as Jesus promised, in the

truth of Christ and in the light that He brought us: "He will teach you all things, and bring to your remembrance all that I have said to you" (John 14:26).

This action of the Holy Spirit in the Church is varied and assorted. I told you before that Christ was consecrated Messiah and Pontiff by an ineffable anointing of the Holy Spirit, and with a similar anointing Christ consecrates those whom He wishes to make participants in His priestly power, in order to continue in the earth His sanctifying mission: "Receive the Holy Spirit" (John 20:22). The Holy Spirit appointed the bishops to govern the Church (Acts 20:28); it is the Holy Spirit who speaks through their mouths and gives value to their witness (see John 15:26; Acts 15:28; 20:22–28). In the same way, the sacraments, authentic means that Christ placed in the hands of His ministers to transmit life to souls, are never conferred without preceding or accompanying the invocation of the Holy Spirit. It is He who makes the waters of Baptism fruitful: "Unless one is born of water and the Spirit, he cannot enter the kingdom of God" (John 3:5). "God," adds St. Paul, "saved us ... by the washing of regeneration and renewal in the Holy Spirit" (Tit. 3:5). That same Spirit is "given" to us in the sacrament of Confirmation, to be the anointing that should make the Christian a fearless soldier of Jesus Christ; it is He who confers on us in that sacrament the fullness of the Christian condition and clothes us with the strength of Christ. To the Holy Spirit, as the Eastern Church makes clear to us above all, is attributed the change that makes the bread and wine the Body and Blood of Jesus Christ. Sins are forgiven in the sacrament of penance by the Holy Spirit (see John 20:22–23). In the anointing of the sick, He is asked "by His grace to cure the sick of their infirmities and guilt." In marriage, finally, the Holy Spirit is also invoked so that Christian spouses may, by their lives, imitate the union that exists between Christ and His Church.

Do you see how lively, deep, and unceasing is the action of the Holy Spirit in the Church? We can well say with St. Paul that He is the "Spirit of life" (Rom. 8:2); a truth that the Church repeats in the Symbol when she expresses her faith in the "life-giving Spirit": *Dominum et vivificantem.* It is truly the soul of the Church, the vital principle that animates the supernatural society, that governs it and unites its various members to one another and gives them spiritual vigor and beauty.

In the early days of the Church, His action was much more visible than in our day. Thus it suited the designs of Providence, for it was necessary that the Church should be firmly established, manifesting to the eyes of the pagan world the luminous signs of the divinity of its founder, its origin and its mission. These signs, fruit of the outpouring of the Holy Spirit, were admirable, and we still marvel when we read the account of the beginnings of the Church. The Spirit descended upon those whom Baptism made disciples of Christ and filled them with charisms as varied as they were astonishing: the grace of miracles, the gift of prophecy, the gift of tongues and a thousand other extraordinary favors granted to the first Christians so that, on contemplating the Church adorned with such a profusion of magnificent gifts, it would be clearly seen that it was truly the Church of Jesus. Read the First Letter of St. Paul to the Corinthians, and you will see with what delight the apostle enumerates the marvels of which He Himself was a witness. In each enumeration of these varied gifts he adds: "All these are inspired by one and the same Spirit" (1 Cor. 12:11), because He is love, and love is the source of all the gifts in the same Spirit. It is he who makes fruitful this Church, which Jesus redeemed with His blood and willed to be "holy and without blemish" (Eph 5:27).[52]

Let us now specify, with all theological rigor and accuracy, in what sense the Holy Spirit is and can be called the soul of the Church.

It is evident, first of all, that the Holy Spirit is not and cannot be the substantial form of the Church in the sense that the soul of the human body is. The soul, as is known and has been defined by the Church, is the substantial form of the human body which it animates (see Dz 481). As such a form, it has the mission of informing—that is, of giving the body its being as a human body, of forming with it one and the same being, determined specifically and numerically by the soul itself. It is clear that the Holy Spirit cannot be the soul of the Church in this sense, because, apart from the fact that the form is part of a determined compound, and God cannot be part of anything or anyone, it would follow that the Church would have a substantively divine being, since it would form one and the same substance with its form; that is to say, that the Church would be God, which is heretical and absurd.

Besides the function of informing, or giving the body the being it has and forming with it a substantive unity, the soul possesses and develops other functions, such as unifying the parts of the body among themselves, vivifying them, and moving them, and

[52] Marmion, *Jesus Christ, life of the soul*, I, 6, 3.

this the Holy Spirit as the soul of the Church can and does do. Let us consider this in detail.[53]

The Holy Spirit Unifies the Church

In the Church there is a great diversity of members. There is hierarchical diversity, charismatic diversity, sanctifying diversity. There are those who rule and those who obey, and among those who rule there are those who do so with universal power and those who do so with limited power: pope, bishops, priests. There are also those who have different charisms: some work miracles, others prophesy, others teach. There are also different degrees of holiness: some possess sanctifying grace in its most exalted manifestations; others are less holy, and there are those who barely have what is indispensable for salvation, and even less. There are very holy saints, there are the just who limit themselves to being in a state of grace, and there are sinners.

In spite of so much diversity, there exists among them all an intimate unity. Christ asked for it for those who were to be His members: "That they may all be one; even as thou, Father, art in me, and I in thee, that they also may be in us.... The glory which thou hast given me I have given to them, that they may be one even as we are one" (John 17:21–22). It is noteworthy that the unity that Christ asks for His Church bears a resemblance to that which He and the Father possess.

Christ and the Father have many reasons for union. They possess the same divine nature, numerically identical; the former is united to the latter, because He is His subsistent Word. But the Holy Spirit gives a special reason for the union between the two Persons. In the trinitarian mystery, the Father and the Son, compared to each other, are distinct: the Father begets and the Son is begotten. Compared with the Holy

---

[53] E. Sauras, *El Cuerpo místico de Cristo* (Madrid: BAC, 1956), 752, where this question is studied extensively and profoundly. We have included, in part, pages 781–784.

Spirit, they constitute the same identical breathing principle. They are one in the expiratory action, from which the third Person proceeds.

It is significant that love is appropriated to the third Person and that Christ desires that the union that must exist between those who form His Mystical Body be a union of love: "I made known to them thy name, and I will make it known, that the love with which thou hast loved me may be in them, and I in them" (John 17:26). All this seems to mean that the union that exists in the Church, a union similar to that between the Father and the Son, must resemble that which exists between them in their relationship with the Holy Spirit. Love unifies the Church, and the Holy Spirit unifies her by love, and so, the members of the Mystical Body are unified where the Father and the Son are unified—that is, in the Holy Spirit. This is something that St. Paul says very clearly when, after naming the many charisms and the many offices that exist in Christian society, he writes: "For by one Spirit we were all baptized into one body—Jews or Greeks, slaves or free—and all were made to drink of one Spirit" (1 Cor. 12:13).

The Holy Spirit Enlivens the Church

The Church is a living being, in the authentic sense of the word. It is a true Mystical Body, and the mystical or supernatural character is founded on a divine and life-giving element.

All societies constituted by men have life in a certain sense: they move, they progress, they perfect themselves, but in reality, the principle that animates them is outside them, it is their end, and the end is an extrinsic cause. This does not rhyme with the definition of life, which is that of movement proceeding from within. Let it not be said that the life of societies comes from the individuals who constitute them; these are the ones who manifest it, they are the members who take advantage of it. The life of these societies proceeds from the end, which is more or less assimilated, which is more or less operative in each of those who go to it, and the end is always an extrinsic cause. Hence it cannot be said with exactitude that societies are living organisms.

The Church, on the other hand, is, because it has an intrinsic life-giving principle. The Holy Spirit is not only end and goal; He is also the animating principle of the Church, an immanent or internal principle, although not a formal one. The Spirit is a living and vivifying principle. He intervened in the appearance of Christ on earth, actively impregnating Mary, and He intervenes in the birth of the Church. The day of Pentecost was the day of the official proclamation of the society established by Christ, and on that day Mary and the Holy Spirit appear in the official birth of this society, as in the birth of Christ. The Church is born with her Baptism, as we are born with ours, and the Baptism of the Church was that of Pentecost. Referring to this day, Jesus said to His disciples when He said goodbye to them moments before ascending to Heaven: "John baptized with water, but before many days you shall be baptized with the Holy Spirit" (Acts 1:5). It is true that Christ instituted His Church before the Ascension, but the living faith of the Church is given on the day the Spirit descended on Mary and the apostles.

It is also the Holy Spirit who vivifies each of the members of the Church. In Him we are baptized; He gives us, therefore, the vital principle, which is the divine grace, and by giving it to us makes us children of God: "All who are led by the Spirit of God are sons of God. For you did not receive the spirit of slavery to fall back into fear, but you have received the spirit of sonship. When we cry, 'Abba! Father!' it is the Spirit himself bearing witness with our spirit that we are children of God, and if children, then heirs, heirs of God and fellow heirs with Christ, provided we suffer with him in order that we may also be glorified with him" (Rom. 8:14-16).

It is the Spirit who gives life to the Church and to each of her members, and He gives it not from without, as the end gives it to earthly societies, but from within, as the soul gives it. When we say that the Holy Spirit begets and vivifies, we do not mean that He does this without penetrating into those who are begotten and vivified. He is in them, He dwells in them, because, in leaving them the vivifying grace, He remains with the other two Divine Persons, as we shall see later on.

The Holy Spirit Moves and Governs the Church

Finally, as the soul moves and governs the body, so the Holy Spirit governs the Church. To govern, it is necessary to know and to love, and it is the Holy Spirit who instills knowledge of the supernatural (faith) and who gives divine love to Christians (charity). He also intervenes, as we have already said, in the appointment of the hierarchs (see Acts 20:28), and when the apostle points out the various offices in the Church, he adds: "All these are inspired by one and the same Spirit, who apportions to each one individually as he wills" (1 Cor. 12:11).

There is no need to add more. If He is the one who governs and moves the members of the Mystical Body of Christ, who unifies them, who vivifies them, and if He does all this from within, dwelling in each member and in the whole Body, we must conclude by saying that He performs authentic functions of a soul. The genius of St. Augustine had already intuited this truth when He wrote resolutely: "What is the soul to the body of man, is the Holy Spirit to the Body of Christ which is the Church."[54]

The official Magisterium of the Church has also applied to the Holy Spirit the expression "soul of the Church" in the sense just explained. See, for example, the following text of Pius XII in his masterly encyclical *Mystici Corporis*:

[54] "Quod anima est hominis corpori, Spiritus Sanctus est corpori Christi, id est Ecclesiae": St. Augustine, Serm. 186 de tempore: PL 38, 1231.

To this Spirit of Christ, as to an invisible principle, it must also be attributed that all the parts are intimately united, both among themselves and with their exalted head, being as it is all in the head, all in the body, all in each of the members; in which He is present, assisting them in many ways, according to their various offices and functions, according to the greater or lesser degree of spiritual perfection they enjoy. He, with His heavenly breath of life, is to be considered as the principle of all vital and salutary action in all parts of the Body. He, although present by Himself in all the members and working in them with His divine influence, makes use of the ministry of the superiors to act in the inferiors. He, finally, while He daily begets new members to the Church by the action of His grace, refuses to dwell with sanctifying grace in the totally separated members. Which presence and operation of the Spirit of Christ was briefly and concisely signified by our most wise predecessor Leo XIII, of immortal memory, in his encyclical letter *Divinum illud*, in these words: "Suffice it to affirm this: that while Christ is the head of the Church, the Holy Spirit is her soul" [ASS 29 (1896–1897) 650]."[55]

The Second Vatican Council, for its part, once again enshrined this magnificent doctrine in the dogmatic constitution of the Church with the following words:

> The Head of this body is Christ.... So that we might be continually renewed in Him (see Eph. 4:22), He granted us to share in His Spirit, who, being one in the

---

[55] Pío XII, *Mystici Corporis*, 26: AAS 35 (1943) 219–220.

Head and in the members, so vivifies the whole Body, unites it and moves it, that His office could be compared by the Holy Fathers to the function exercised by the principle of life or the soul in the human body.[56]

After this quick glance at the presence and action of the Holy Spirit in the whole Church of Christ, let us now look at that which corresponds to each of its members in particular. But this requires a separate chapter.

[56] Second Vatican Council, Dogmatic Constitution Lumen gentium, 7.

CHAPTER 6

The Holy Spirit In Us

IN THIS CHAPTER we address one of the holiest and most sublime themes of all sacred theology: the indwelling of the Holy Spirit in the soul justified by grace.

It is necessary, first of all, to have very clear ideas about the intimate nature of sanctifying grace, which is the basis and foundation of the indwelling of the Holy Spirit and of the whole Blessed Trinity in the justified soul. For this reason we are going to dwell on the exposition of the fundamental principles of the theology of grace, even at the risk of incurring in a small digression, which we judge to be absolutely necessary and very practical and profitable.

I. Sanctifying Grace

We will briefly explain its nature and the main effects it produces in our souls.

WHAT IS GRACE?

Sanctifying grace can be defined as a supernatural gift infused by God into our souls to give us a true and real participation in His own divine nature, to make us His children and heirs of glory.

We will explain the definition word by word to better grasp its splendid reality.

a) It is a gift. Grace is an immense gift of God, a total and absolutely free gift that no one has the right to claim from a purely natural point of view. Once in gratuitous possession of this immense gift, we can already negotiate with it and merit new increases of grace and the same eternal glory, as we will see below. Before possessing grace, absolutely no one can merit it, although we can humbly ask God for it with confident and persevering prayer. It is a beautiful and consoling theological aphorism to say that "to him who does what he can (with the help of the same prevenient grace), God does not deny His grace."

b) It is a supernatural gift. Supernatural means that it is above nature, so much above that grace is a divine reality, infinitely superior to all created or creatable nature.

In fact, if we scale the set of all the creatures created by God in their different degrees, known to us by natural light and by divine revelation, we find the following five, from the lowest to the highest:

1. Minerals. They exist, but do not live.

2. Vegetables. They live, but do not feel or understand.

3. Animals. They live and feel, but do not understand or think.

4. Man. He is, as St. Gregory says, a kind of microcosm (a small world), which summarizes all other created beings: he exists, like the minerals; he lives, like the plants; he feels, like the animals, and he understands, like the angels.

5. Angels. Pure spirits, they have neither body nor any mixture of matter, and are, therefore,

naturally superior to man, since they are nearer
to the very being of God.

To which of these degrees or categories does habitual or sanctifying grace belong? To none of them, since it transcends and surpasses them all. Grace, as we will explain shortly, is a divine reality which, by the same token, belongs to the plane of divinity and is a thousand times above all created beings, including the angels themselves. It is an absolutely supernatural reality—that is to say, it is above, surpasses, and transcends all created or creatable nature. That is why the smallest participation of sanctifying grace is worth infinitely more than the entire universal creation, that is, the whole of all the beings created by God that have existed, exist, and will exist until the end of time.[57]

c) Infused by God. Only God, the author of the supernatural order, can infuse it into the soul. All the creatures together in the universe can never produce the smallest participation in the very nature of God, which is precisely what sanctifying grace communicates to us.

d) In our souls. Grace is a spiritual reality that resides in the soul, not in the body. Because it is spiritual, it cannot be seen with the eyes, nor touched, nor heard. Neither can thought or love be seen or touched, and yet it is an authentic reality that we think and love.

e) To give us a true and real participation in His own divine nature. It is the first and greatest prerogative of God's grace, which we will explain in detail below when we speak of the effects of grace on our souls.

---

[57] That is why St. Thomas says that "the good of grace of a single individual is greater than the natural good of the whole universe": STh I–II, q. 113 a. 9 ad 2.

f) It makes us true children of God. This is a necessary consequence of the fact that sanctifying grace makes us participants in the very nature of God. Without this participation we would only be God's creatures, but in no way His children.

Indeed, in order to be a father it is necessary to transmit one's own specific nature to another being. The sculptor who sculpts a statue is not the father of that inanimate work, but only the author. On the other hand, the authors of our days are truly our fathers in the natural order, because they really transmitted to us, by way of generation, their own human nature.

It is true that God does not transmit to us by grace His own divine nature by natural generation, as the Father transmits it to the Son in the bosom of the Most Blessed Trinity, but in a partial form and by way of adoption, not natural. But we must beware of believing that this divine adoption by means of grace is of the same nature as human adoptions; by no means. When a child orphaned of father and mother is legally adopted by a charitable family, he receives from it a series of goods and advantages, among which stand out the surname of the adopting family and the right to the goods that are assigned to him in inheritance. But there is one thing they do not give him, nor can they ever give him: the blood of the family. That poor child has the blood he received from his natural parents, but by no means that of his adoptive parents. On the other hand, when God adopts us by grace, he not only gives us the surname of the divine family (children of God) and the right to the future inheritance (Heaven), but He communicates to us in a very real and true way His own divine nature. Using metaphorical language, since God has no blood, but language which nevertheless contains a sublime reality at its core, we could say that grace is a transfusion of divine blood into our souls. By virtue of this divine transfusion, this divine grafting, the soul becomes a participant in the very life of God in such a way that it not only gives us the right to call ourselves children of God, but actually makes us such. This is why John the Evangelist exclaims in amazement: "See what love the Father has given us, that we should be called children of God; and so we are" (1 John 3:1).

The Apostle Paul writes in his Letter to the Romans: "For you did not receive the spirit of slavery to fall back into fear, but you have received the spirit of sonship. When we cry, 'Abba! Father!' it is the Spirit himself bearing witness with our spirit that we are children of God, and if children, then heirs, heirs of God and fellow heirs with Christ" (Rom. 8:15–17).

By grace, then, we are truly children of God by adoption, but by a kind of intrinsic adoption, which really incorporates us into the family of God as true children.

g) It makes us heirs of Heaven. This is another natural and obligatory consequence of our adoptive divine filiation. St. Paul reminds us of this in the words we have just quoted: "If children, then heirs" (Rom 8:17).

But how different is the adoptive filiation of grace from purely human or legal adoptions! Among men, children inherit only when the father dies, and the more heirs there are, the lesser the inheritance of each. But our Father lives and will live forever, and with Him we will possess such an inheritance that, in spite of the immense number of participants, it will never experience the least diminution, for this inheritance, at least in its principal aspects, is rigorously infinite. It is the same God, one in essence and triune in Persons, contemplated, loved, and enjoyed with ineffable and intoxicating delights, which in this earthly life we cannot even imagine. All the inner riches of the Divinity, all that constitutes God's happiness itself and gives an infinite and eternal delight, are the unfathomable perfections of the Divinity. Finally, God will place at our disposal all His external goods: His honor, His glory, His dominions, His kingship, and all the created goods that exist in the entire universe: "All are yours; and you are Christ's; and Christ is God's" (1 Cor. 3:22–23). All this will provide the soul with inexplicable happiness and joy, which will fulfill fully, in overflowing abundance, all its aspirations and longings.

All this the soul in grace will receive as an inheritance due by way of justice: it has a right to it. Grace, as we have explained above, is entirely gratuitous, an immense gift of God that absolutely no one can merit from the purely natural point of view; but, once possessed, it gives us the capacity to merit Heaven by way of righteousness. There is a perfect parallel and correspondence between grace and Heaven, as there is also between mortal sin and Hell. Grace is like Heaven in potential. There is between grace and Heaven only a difference of degree, not an essential difference: it is the same supernatural life in the initial state or in the consummated state. The child does not differ specifically from the mature man; he is an adult in seed form. The same is true of grace and glory. That is why St. Thomas was able to write with all theological accuracy that "grace is nothing other than a beginning of glory in us."[58]

EFFECTS OF SANCTIFYING GRACE

a) It divinizes us, making us participants in the very nature of God. This is the first and greatest of the effects that sanctifying grace produces in our souls, and the root and foundation of all the others.

We could hardly believe it if it were not clearly and expressly stated in divine revelation. St. Peter the Apostle says that God "has granted to us his precious and very great promises, that through

---

[58] See STh II–II, q. 24 a. 3 ad 2.

these you may escape from the corruption that is in the world because of passion, and become partakers of the divine nature" (2 Pet. 1:4). The Holy Fathers and modern exegesis itself have seen in these words a clear and manifest allusion to sanctifying grace,[59] and the Church joyfully exclaims in her official liturgy: "Christ ascended into Heaven to make us sharers in His divinity."[60]

Does this mean that man is made substantially divine by grace in the pantheistic sense of the expression? It would be a great error and true heresy to say so. There is not and cannot be a substantial change of human nature in the divine substance. It is only a matter of an analogical and accidental participation by virtue of which man, without ceasing to be such, becomes a participant in the divine nature insofar as it is possible for a simple creature.[61] The Holy Fathers often use the image of an iron put into a fiery furnace: the iron does not thereby lose its own iron nature, but acquires the properties of fire and becomes incandescent like it. In a similar way, the soul, on receiving the grace of God, continues to be substantially a human soul, but it receives a true and real participation in the very nature of God, because grace makes it capable of knowing and loving God as He knows and loves Himself. Since the nature of God consists precisely in knowing and loving the divine, to participate in this

---

[59] "The formula physis divina," writes a modern exegete, "designates the Divine Being, the Divinity itself. It is the divine nature itself as opposed to all that is not God. St. Peter's lapidary formula is bold and at the same time clear, since it clarifies the most splendid effect of sanctifying grace.... The Christian participates in the divine nature itself, that is to say, in the whole accumulation of perfections contained in a formal-eminent way in the divine essence": J. Salguero, "Segunda epístola de san Pedro", in Profesores de la Uiv. Pont. de Salamanca, *Biblia comentada*, VII (Madrid: BAC, 1965), 156.

[60] Preface of the feast of the Ascension of the Lord.

[61] We have explained all this at length in our *Theology of Christian Perfection* (Madrid: BAC, 1968), n. 86. In the pre–1968 editions it was n. 32.

knowledge and love is to participate really and truly of its own divine nature. The soul in grace resembles God precisely insofar as it is God—that is, not only as a living and intelligent being, but in that which makes God different from everything else: its very divinity. It is impossible for a creature, human or angelic, to reach a greater height than that to which it is raised by sanctifying grace, except for the personal or hypostatic union, which is proper and exclusive to Christ.

The dignity of a soul in grace is so great that before it all the greatness of the earth vanishes like smoke. What does everything created mean before a beggar covered with rags who carries in his soul the treasure of sanctifying grace? There is more distance between that beggar and a soul in mortal sin (which lacks grace) than there is between that beggar in grace and the greatest of the canonized saints, and even that between him and the Blessed Virgin Mary. To such a remarkable height does the simple possession of sanctifying grace raise us! It makes us surpass the frontiers of all natural creation, making us reach, in its eagle's flight, the very plane of divinity: God Himself as He is in Himself.

The devil promised our first parents in Paradise that, if they ate of the forbidden tree, "they would be like gods" (Gen. 3:5). "It is Jesus Christ," says Malebranche, "who, through grace, fulfills in us the magnificent promise of the devil."[62]

b) It makes us brothers of Christ and co-heirs with Him. This is the third affirmation of St. Paul in the text of the Letter to the Romans quoted above, "heirs of God and fellow heirs with Christ" (Rom. 8:17), and this relationship derives immediately from the other two

---

[62] Quoted by Father Sertillanges in *Catecismo de los incrédulos* (Barcelona: Políglota, 1934), 211.

preceding ones. For, as St. Augustine says, "he who says our Father to the Father of Christ, what does He say to Christ our brother?"[63]

By the very fact that grace communicates to us a participation in the divine life that Christ possesses in all its fullness, we must become His brothers and sisters. He willed to become our brother according to humanity "in order to make us His brothers according to divinity."[64] "Those whom he foreknew," St. Paul writes, "he also predestined to be conformed to the image of his Son, in order that he might be the first-born among many brethren" (Rom. 8:29). Certainly we are not brothers of Christ according to nature, nor are we sons of God in the same way that He is. Christ is the firstborn among His brethren, but also the only begotten Son of the Father. In the order of nature He is the only Son, but in the order of adoption and grace He is our elder brother, as well as our Head and the cause of our health.

For this reason, the Father deigns to look upon us as one with His Son. He loves us as Himself, considers Him as our brother, and confers on us a title to His own inheritance. We are co-heirs of Christ. He has a natural right to the divine inheritance, since He is the Son "whom he appointed the heir of all things, through whom also he created the world" (Heb. 1:2). Now "it was fitting that he, for whom and by whom all things exist, in bringing many sons to glory, should make the pioneer of their salvation perfect through suffering. For he who sanctifies and those who are sanctified have all one origin. That is why he is not ashamed to call them brethren, saying, 'I will proclaim thy name to my brethren, in the midst of the congregation I will praise thee'" (Heb. 2:10–12). For this reason, these brothers of Christ are to share with Him the love and the inheritance of the Heavenly Father. God has modeled us on Christ; we are with Him the children of the same Father who

---

[63] St. Augustine, In Io. tr. 21, 3: PL 35, 1565.
[64] See preface to the feast of the Ascension.

is in Heaven. Ultimately, everything will come to an end, fulfilling the supreme desire of Christ: that we may be one with Him, as He is one with His Heavenly Father.

c) It infuses us with the virtues and gifts of the Holy Spirit.
Sanctifying grace is a supernatural quality, which is infused into the very essence of our soul as a static, habitual, and not immediately operative element. In order to act supernaturally, as our elevation to the supernatural order by grace itself demands, we need operative faculties of a strictly supernatural order that enable us to perform in a connatural and effortless way the supernatural acts proper to our condition as children of God. Such are the infused virtues and the gifts of the Holy Spirit, which are always infused into us together with sanctifying grace, of which they are inseparable and of which they constitute its operative or dynamic element. We will return to this at length in its corresponding place.[65]

II. The Trinitarian Indwelling of the Soul

Sanctifying grace, as we have already said, gives us a true and real participation in the very nature of God, and in this sense it can properly and accurately be called divine. However, it is quite evident that it is not God Himself, but a reality created by God to make us participants in His own divine nature in a mysterious, though very real and true, way.

But this created reality, which is sanctifying grace, always carries with it, inseparably, another absolutely divine and uncreated reality, which is none other than God Himself, one and triune, who comes to dwell in the very depths of our souls.

---

[65] With the exception of faith and hope, which can subsist without grace, although in a formless way—that is, without any vitality of a supernatural meritorious order.

We are going to study this august reality with the maximum amplitude that the framework of our work allows us.[66]

EXISTENCE

The indwelling of the Most Holy Trinity in the soul of the just is one of the truths most clearly manifested in the New Testament.[67] With an insistence that clearly shows the sovereign importance of this mystery, the sacred text returns again and again to instill in us this sublime truth.

Let us recall some of the most distinguished testimonies:

> If a man loves me, he will keep my word, and my Father will love him, and we will come to him and make our home with him (John 14:23).

> God is love, and he who abides in love abides in God, and God abides in him (1 John 4:16).

> Do you not know that you are God's temple and that God's Spirit dwells in you? If any one destroys God's temple, God will destroy him. For God's temple is holy, and that temple you are (1 Cor. 3:16–17).

> Do you not know that your body is a temple of the Holy Spirit within you, which you have from God? You are not your own (1 Cor. 6:19).

> For we are the temple of the living God (2 Cor. 6:16).

---

[66] We reiterate here what we have written in our *Theology of Christian Perfection*, n. 40–44.

[67] As is well known, although in the Old Testament there are some traces and vestiges of the trinitarian mystery, especially in the doctrine of the "Spirit of God" and of "Wisdom," nevertheless, the full revelation of the mystery of the intimate life of God was reserved for the New Testament.

> Guard the truth that has been entrusted to you by the
> Holy Spirit who dwells within us (2 Tim. 1:14).

As can be seen, Sacred Scripture employs various formulas to express the same truth: God dwells within the soul in grace. Preferably this indwelling is attributed to the Holy Spirit, not because there is a special presence of the Holy Spirit that is not common to the Father and the Son, but by a very convenient appropriation, since this is the great work of God's love for man and the Holy Spirit is the essential Love in the bosom of the Most Holy Trinity.[68]

The Holy Fathers, especially St. Augustine, have beautiful pages commenting on the ineffable fact of the divine indwelling in the soul of the just.

NATURE

Much has been written and discussed by theologians about the nature of the indwelling of the Divine Persons in the soul of the just.

There are many opinions, and perhaps none of them can give us an entirely satisfactory explanation of the mysterious way in which the real presence of the Divine Persons is realized in the soul of the just person. In any case, for a life of piety and progress toward perfection, more than the way in which it is carried out, what matters is the fact of indwelling, in which all Catholic theologians absolutely agree.

---

[68] Some theologians, such as Lessio, Petau, Tomassino, Scheeben, and so on, thought so; but the vast majority affirm the contrary doctrine, which is clearly deduced from the data of faith and the doctrine of the Church (Dz 281). See J. B. Terrien, *La gracia y la gloria* (Madrid, Fax, 1943) lib. 6, c. 6, append. 5; B. Froget, *De l'habitation du Saint Esprit dans les âmes justes d'après la doctrine de Saint Thomas d'Aquin* (Paris: P. Lethielleux, 1900), 442; P. Galtier, *L'habitation en nous des trois Personnes* (Rome: Pont. Univ. Gregoriana, 1950), c. 1.

Disregarding, then, the various theories formulated to explain the mode of divine indwelling, we will point out how the presence of indwelling differs from the other presences of God that theology points out.

In fact, up to five completely different presences of God can be distinguished:

1. Personal and hypostatic presence. It is the proper and exclusive presence of Jesus the Christ-man. In Him the Divine Person of the Word does not reside as in a temple, but constitutes His own personality, even as a man. By virtue of the hypostatic union, the Christ-man is a Divine Person, in no way a human person.

2. Eucharistic presence. God is present in the Eucharist in a special way that only occurs in the Eucharist. It is the eucharistic *ubi*, which, although affecting only the body of Christ in a direct and immediate way, also affects indirectly the three Divine Persons of the Blessed Trinity: the Word by His personal union with the humanity of Christ, and the Father and the Holy Spirit by the circuminsession or mutual presence of the three Divine Persons among themselves, which makes them absolutely inseparable.

3. Presence of vision. God is present everywhere, as we will see later, but He does not let Himself be seen everywhere. The Beatific Vision in Heaven can be considered as a special presence of God distinct from the others. In Heaven God allows Himself to be seen.

4. Presence of immensity. One of the attributes of God is His immensity, by virtue of which God is really present everywhere, and no creature or place can exist where God is not found:

   a) By essence, inasmuch as God is giving being to everything that exists without resting for an instant, in a manner similar to the way the power plant is ceaselessly sending the electricity that keeps the light bulb on. If God were to suspend for a single instant His conserving action on any being, that being would ipso facto disappear into nothingness, just as the electric lamp is instantly extinguished when we cut off the current. In this sense, God is present even in a soul in mortal sin and in the devil himself, who could not exist without this divine presence.

   b) By presence, inasmuch as God has all created beings continually before His eyes, and none of them can escape His divine gaze for a single instant.

   c) By power, inasmuch as God has all creatures subject to His power. With a single word He created them and with a single word He could annihilate them.

5. Presence of indwelling. It is the special presence that God, one and triune, establishes in the soul justified by grace. How does this presence of inhabitation differ from the general presence of immensity? First of all, it must be said that the special

presence of indwelling presupposes and preexists the general presence of immensity, without which it would not be possible. But it adds to this general presence two fundamental things, namely: divine paternity and friendship; the first, founded on sanctifying grace, the second on charity.

a) Paternity. As we have already said in speaking of sanctifying grace, properly speaking, it cannot be said that God is Father of creatures in the purely natural order. It is true that they have all come from His creative hands, but this fact constitutes God the Author or Creator of them all; it in no way makes Him their Father. The artist who carves a statue in a piece of wood or marble is the author of the statue, but in no way its father. To be a father it is necessary to transmit one's own life — that is, one's own specific nature — to another living being of the same species. Therefore, if God wanted to be our Father as well as our Creator, it was necessary for Him to transmit to us His own divine nature in all its fullness — and this is the case with Jesus Christ, Son of God by nature — or, at least, a real and true participation in it: and this is the case of the justified soul. By virtue of sanctifying grace, which gives us a mysterious but very real and true participation in the divine nature itself, the justified soul becomes truly a daughter of God, by an intrinsic adoption far superior to human adoptions, which are purely juridical and extrinsic, and from that moment,

God, who already resided in the soul by His general presence of immensity, begins to be in it as Father and to look upon it as His true daughter. This is the first aspect of the presence of indwelling, incomparably superior, as we can see, to the simple presence of immensity. The presence of immensity is common to everything that exists (even to stones and to the demons themselves). That of indwelling, on the other hand, is proper and exclusive to the children of God. It always presupposes sanctifying grace and, therefore, could not be given without it.

b) Friendship. But sanctifying grace never goes alone. It carries with it the marvelous cortege of the infused virtues, among which supernatural charity stands out as the most important and principal. Charity establishes a true and mutual friendship between God and mankind: it is its very essence.[69] Therefore, when supernatural charity is infused into the soul, together with sanctifying grace, God begins to be in it in a way that is entirely new: He is no longer simply the author, but also a true friend. This is the second endearing aspect of divine indwelling.

The intimate presence of God, one and triune, as Father and Friend: this is the colossal fact that constitutes the very essence of the indwelling of the Most Holy Trinity in the soul justified by grace and charity.

[69] See STh II–II, q. 23 a.1.

PURPOSE

The trinitarian indwelling in our souls has a very high purpose, as it could not be otherwise. It is the great gift of God, the first and greatest of all possible gifts, since it gives us the real and true possession of the infinite being of God Himself. Sanctifying grace itself, though a gift of inestimable value, is worth infinitely less than divine indwelling. The latter receives in theology the name of uncreated grace, as opposed to habitual or sanctifying grace, which is designated by the name of created grace. There is a gulf between a creature, however perfect it may be, and the Creator Himself.

Inhabitation is equivalent in the Christian to hypostatic union in the Person of Christ, although it is not the latter, but habitual grace, which formally constitutes us as adopted children of God. Sanctifying grace penetrates and formally imbues our soul, divinizing it. But divine indwelling is like the incarnation or insertion into our souls of the absolutely divine, of the very being of God as He is in Himself, one in essence and triune in Persons.

There are two main purposes of the divine indwelling in our souls:

First, the Most Holy Trinity dwells in our souls to make us participants in His intimate divine life and to transform us into God. The intimate life of God consists, as we have already said, in the procession of the Divine Persons, the Word, from the Father by way of intellectual generation; and the Holy Spirit, from the Father and the Son by way of affective origin, and in the infinite pleasure that the Divine Persons experience in them among themselves.

Now, however incredible this statement may seem, the trinitarian indwelling of our souls tends, as the supreme goal, to make us participants in the mystery of the intimate divine life, associating us with Him and transforming us into God, insofar as this is possible for a simple creature. Let us listen to St. John of the Cross explaining this incredible marvel:

This breathing in of the air is an ability that the soul says it will be given there in the communication of the Holy Spirit, who, in the manner of breathing in, with His divine aspiration very subtly raises the soul and informs and enables it to breathe into God the same aspiration of love that the Father breathes into the Son, and the Son into the Father, which is the same Holy Spirit, who breathes into it in the Father and the Son in the said transformation, to unite it with Himself. For it would not be true and total transformation if the soul were not transformed into the three Persons of the Most Holy Trinity in a revealed and manifest degree.

This aspiration of the Holy Spirit in the soul, with which God transforms it into Himself, is such a high and delicate and profound delight for it, that it is not necessary to say it by mortal tongue, nor can the human understanding as such reach anything of it....

It is not to be considered impossible that the soul should be able to do so high a thing, that the soul should aspire in God as God aspires in it by mode of participation. It is a work of understanding, knowledge and love. For since God has done it the mercy of uniting it in the Most Holy Trinity, in which the soul is made deiform and God by participation, what incredible thing is it that it also works its work of understanding, knowledge, and love, or, to put it better, has it worked in the Trinity together with it as the Trinity itself? But by way of communication and participation, God working it in the soul itself; for this is to be transformed into the three Persons in power and wisdom and love, and in this the soul is like God, and so that it might come to this He created it in His image and likeness....

> O souls bred for these great things, and for them called, what do you do? How are you entertained? Your pretensions are baseness, and your possessions are miseries; O wretched blindness of your soul's eyes, for you are blind to so much light and deaf to so many great voices, not seeing that while you seek greatness and glory you remain miserable and low, ignorant, and unworthy of so many goods![70]

So much for St. John of the Cross. Truly, the final apostrophe of the sublime mystic of Fontiver is fully justified. Before the sovereign perspective of our total transformation in God, the Christian should radically despise all the miseries of the earth and dedicate himself with uncontainable ardor to intensify more and more his trinitarian life until he soars little by little to the highest summits of mystical union with God.

Let it not be thought, however, that this total transformation into God of which the experimental mystics speak as the supreme crowning of the trinitarian indwelling has a pantheistic sense of absorption of one's own personality in the stream of divine life. Nothing could be further from this. Pantheistic union is not properly union, but absolute negation of the union, since one of the two terms, the creature, disappears when it is absorbed by God. Mystical union is not this. The soul transformed into God never loses its own created personality. St. Thomas gives the extraordinarily graphic and expressive example of red-hot iron, which, without losing its own iron nature, acquires the properties of fire and becomes fire by participation.[71]

[70] St. John of the Cross, *Spiritual Canticle*, 39, 3–4 and 7.
[71] See STh I–II, q. 112 a. 1; I, q.8 a.1; I q. 44 a. 1, etc.

Commenting on this divine transformation based on the image of the burning iron, Fr. Ramière rightly observes:

> It is true that in the scorched iron there is the likeness of fire, but it is not such that the most skillful painter can reproduce it with the most vivid colors; it can only result from the presence and action of the fire itself. The presence of fire and the combustion of iron are two different things; for the former is a way of being of iron, and the latter a relation of iron to a foreign substance. But the two things, however distinct they may be, are inseparable one from the other; fire cannot be united to iron without burning it, and the combustion of iron cannot result except from its union with fire.
>
> Thus, the just soul possesses in itself a holiness distinct from the Holy Spirit; but it is inseparable from the presence of the Holy Spirit in that soul, and is therefore infinitely superior to the highest holiness that could be attained by a soul in which the Holy Spirit does not dwell. The latter soul could not be divinized except morally, by the resemblance of its dispositions to those of God; the Christian, on the contrary, is divinized physically, and, in a certain sense, substantially, since, without becoming one substance and one person with God, he possesses in himself the substance of God and receives the communication of His life.[72]

Secondly, the Most Holy Trinity dwells in our souls to give us the full possession of God and the fruitive enjoyment of the Divine Persons. Two things are contained in this conclusion, which we will examine separately:

---

[72] E. Ramière, *El Corazón de Jesús y la divinización del cristiano* (Bilbao: Desclée, 1936), 229–230.

a) To give us the full possession of God. We said when speaking of the divine presence of immensity that, by virtue of it, God was intimately present in all things, even in the very demons of Hell, by essence, presence and potency, and yet a being who has no other contact with God than that which comes solely from this presence of immensity, properly speaking does not possess God, since this infinite treasure does not belong to him in any way. Let us listen again to Fr. Ramière:

> We can imagine a very poor man next to an immense treasure, without becoming rich by being close to it, for it is not proximity that makes wealth, but the possession of gold. Such is the difference between the righteous soul and the soul of the sinner. The sinner, the damned man himself, has the infinite good at his side and in himself, and yet he remains destitute, because this treasure does not belong to him; whereas the Christian in the state of grace has in himself the Holy Spirit, and with Him the fullness of heavenly graces as a treasure that belongs to him and which he can use as and when he sees fit.
>
> How great is the happiness of the Christian! What a truth, well understood by our understanding, to enlarge our heart! What an influence on our whole life if we had it constantly before our eyes! The persuasion we have of the real presence of the body of Jesus Christ in the ciborium inspires us with the deepest horror at the profanation of that metal vessel. What horror we would have also at the least profanation of our body if we would not lose sight of this dogma of faith, as certain as the first, namely, the real presence in us of the Spirit of Jesus Christ! Is the divine Spirit any less holy than the

sacred flesh of the God-Man? Or do we think that He attaches more importance to the holiness of those golden vessels and material temples than to that of His living temples and spiritual tabernacles?[73]

Nothing, in fact, should fill the Christian with such horror as the possibility of losing this divine treasure through mortal sin. The greatest calamities and misfortunes that we can imagine on the purely human and temporal plane, sickness, slander, loss of all material goods, death of loved ones, etc., are a laughing matter compared to the terrible catastrophe that a single mortal sin represents for the soul. Here the loss is absolute and rigorously infinite.

b) To give us the fruitive enjoyment of the Divine Persons. As astonishing as it is to read it, this is one of the most endearing purposes of the divine indwelling in our souls.

The prince of Catholic theology, St. Thomas Aquinas, wrote in his *Summa Theologiae* these surprising words:

> It is not said that we possess but that which we can freely use and enjoy. Now it is only by sanctifying grace that we have the power to enjoy the Divine Person (*"potestatem fruendi divina persona"*). By the gift of sanctifying grace, the rational creature is perfected, not only to freely use that created gift, but to enjoy the same Divine Person (*"ut ipsa persona divina fruatur"*).[74]

Experiential mystics have verified in practice the profound reality of these words. St. Catherine of Siena, St. Teresa, St. John of the

[73] Ibid., 216–217.
[74] STh I, q. 43 a. 3 c and ad 1.

Cross, Sister Elizabeth of the Trinity, and many others speak of ineffable trinitarian experiences. Their descriptions sometimes baffle speculative theologians, who are perhaps too fond of measuring the greatness of God with the shortness of poor human reason, even when illuminated by faith.[75]

Let us listen to some explicit testimonies of experiential mystics: *St. Teresa:*

> Our good God now wants to remove the scales from her [our soul's] eyes and to make her see and understand something of the mercy that He is doing her, although it is in a strange way; and having entered into that dwelling by intellectual vision, by a certain way of representing the truth, she is shown the Most Holy Trinity, all three Persons, with an inflammation that first comes to her spirit like a cloud of very great clarity, and these distinct Persons, and by a kind news that is given to the soul, she understands with very great truth that all three Persons are one substance and one power and one knowledge and one God. So that what we have by faith is there understood by the soul, we can say, by sight, although it is not seen with the eyes of the body and of the soul, because it is not an imaginary vision. Here all three Persons communicate to her, and speak to her, and

---

[75] In reality, the discrepancies between theologians and mystics are more apparent than real. Mystical experience, by its very ineffability, is not fit to be expressed with poor human concepts. Hence the mystics are constrained to employ inadequate language, which, in the light of simple natural reason, seems excessive and inaccurate, when in reality it still falls far short of the ineffable experience it seeks to express. See, for example, the text of St. John of the Cross that we will quote immediately.

give her to understand those words which the Gospel says that the Lord said, that He and the Father and the Holy Spirit would come to dwell with the soul that loves Him and keeps His commandments. Oh, my God, how different it is to hear these words and believe them than to understand by this way how true they are! Every day this soul is more and more frightened, because it never again seems to her that they are with her, but that she sees, in the way that is said, that they are in the interior of her soul; in the very interior, in a very deep thing, which she cannot say what it is, because she has no letters, she feels in herself this divine company.[76]

St. John of the Cross. We have already quoted in the previous conclusion an extraordinarily expressive text. Let us hear him ponder the ineffable delight that the soul experiences in its sublime trinitarian experience:

From where the delicacy of the delight that is felt in this touch, it is impossible to say; nor would I want to speak of it, lest it be understood that it is no more than what is said, that there are no words to declare such high things of God as in these souls, of which the language itself is to understand it for oneself and feel it for oneself, and to silence it and enjoy it for the one who has it.... And thus it can only be said, and with truth, that it tastes of eternal life; that although in this life it is not perfectly enjoyed as in glory, with all this, this touch of God, it tastes of eternal life.[77]

---

[76] St. Teresa of Jesus, *Seventh Dwelling*, 1, 6–7.
[77] St. John of the Cross, *Flame*, 2, 21.

Sister Elizabeth of the Trinity:

> Here is how I understand being the "house of God":
> living in the bosom of the tranquil Trinity, in my
> inner abyss, in this impregnable fortress of holy recol-
> lection, of which St. John of the Cross speaks.
>
> David sang: "My soul longs, yea, faints for the
> courts of the Lord" (Ps. 84:2). It seems to me that this
> must be the attitude of every soul that withdraws into
> its inner courts to contemplate its God there and to
> come into very close contact with Him. It feels itself
> faint in a divine swoon before the presence of this al-
> mighty Love, of this infinite majesty that dwells
> within it. It is not life that abandons it, it is the soul
> who despises this natural life and who withdraws,
> because it feels that it is not worthy of its rich essence,
> and that it is going to die and disappear in its God.[78]

This is, in all its sublime grandeur, one of the most endearing purposes of the indwelling of the Most Holy Trinity in our souls: to
give us an ineffable experience of the great trinitarian mystery, as a
foretaste and anticipation of eternal Beatitude. The Divine Persons
give themselves to the soul so that we may enjoy them, according
to the astonishing terminology of the Angelic Doctor, fully verified
in practice by the experiential mystics, and although this ineffable
experience undoubtedly constitutes the highest and most sublime
degree of mystical union with God, it does not, however, represent
a favor of an "extraordinary" type in the manner of the graces "freely
given." On the contrary, it enters into the normal development of

---

[78] Sister Elizabeth of the Trinity, "Last retreat of Laudem gloriae, day 16",
can be found in M. M. Philipon, *La doctrina espiritual de Sor Isabel de
la Trinidad* (Bilbao: Desclée, 1965) at the end.

sanctifying grace, and all Christians are called to these heights, and would indeed reach them if they were perfectly faithful to grace and did not paralyze with their continual resistance the progressive sanctifying action of the Holy Spirit. Let us listen to St. Teresa openly proclaiming this doctrine:

> Behold, the Lord invites all; for it is the same truth, let there be no doubt about it. If this invitation were not general, the Lord would not call us all, and even if He did call us, He would not say: "I will give you something to drink" (John 7:37). He could have said, "Come, all of you, and you will lose nothing; and whomsoever I please, I will give you to drink." But since He said, without this condition, to all, I am sure that all who do not tarry on the way will not lack this living water.[79]

It is worthwhile, therefore, to do all we can to prepare ourselves, with God's grace, to enjoy, even in this world, this ineffable trinitarian experience. The most important means to dispose ourselves to this are living faith, ardent charity, profound recollection, and fervent acts of adoration of the Divine Persons dwelling in our souls.

INHABITATION AND SACRAMENTS

As we have just seen, every soul in a state of grace is a temple of the Most Holy Trinity and the tabernacle of the Holy Spirit, as is expressly stated in divine revelation (John 14:23; 1 Cor. 3:16). But this indwelling of the Divine Persons is perfected and takes deeper

---

[79] St. Teresa of Jesus, *The Way of Perfection*, 19, 15; see St. John of the Cross, *Flame*, 2, 27.

root as the degree of sanctifying grace increases in the soul, whatever the cause that has determined this increase may be.[80]

Among the determining causes of this increase are, in the first place, the sacraments, which were instituted by Jesus Christ precisely to give us and increase sanctifying grace.[81] Baptism and penance—for those who receive the latter under the proper conditions after having lost grace through mortal sin—produce divine indwelling in the soul by infusing it with sanctifying grace, from which they are inseparable. The other sacraments, and also penance itself for those who receive it while they are already in the grace of God, produce an increase of grace and a greater establishment or indwelling of the Divine Persons in the soul.

In order to increase grace and perfect the trinitarian indwelling of the soul, it is important to highlight the action of the Eucharist and the sacrament of Confirmation. Let us briefly explain them.

A) THE EUCHARIST

The greatest and most excellent of the seven sacraments instituted by Christ is the Most Holy Eucharist. In it we receive not only grace, but also the very Author of grace, Christ Himself. We receive the water together with the fountain or spring from which it flows.

But what many Christians ignore is that, together with the incarnate Word, we receive in the Eucharist the Father and the Holy Spirit, because the three Divine Persons are absolutely inseparable

---

[80] There are three such causes: the sacraments, which increase grace by their own intrinsic virtue (*ex opere operato*); the practice of the infused virtues, which constitute the supernatural merit (*ex opere operantis*); and prayer, which can increase grace by its impetratory power (as gratuitous almsgiving), independently of the merit it carries with it. We have explained all this at length in our *Theology of Christian Perfection*, n. 284ff, to which we refer the reader who desires further information.

[81] See Dz 844, 849–851.

from each other. Where there is one of them, there are necessarily the other two, by virtue of that ineffable mystery which receives in theology the name of divine circuminsession. This mystery is expressly stated in Sacred Scripture and has been defined by the official Magisterium of the Church. Here are the proofs:

1. Sacred Scripture. Christ Himself says: "I and the Father are one.... The Father is in me and I am in the Father" (John 10:30 and 38). "He who has seen me has seen the Father.... The Father who dwells in me does his works. Believe me that I am in the Father and the Father in me" (John 14:9–11). The same is true, of course, of the Holy Spirit.

2. The Magisterium of the Church. Here are, among many other texts, the explicit words of the Council of Florence: "By reason of this unity, the Father is all in the Son, all in the Holy Spirit; the Son is all in the Father, all in the Holy Spirit; the Holy Spirit is all in the Father, all in the Son. No one precedes another in eternity, or exceeds Him in greatness, or surpasses Him in power" (Dz 704).

This mystery, as we have said, receives in theology the name of circuminsession, which is roughly equivalent to the mutual and reciprocal inhesion of the Divine Persons among themselves. By virtue of it, where one Divine Person is, the other two are also necessarily present, since they are absolutely inseparable from one another and from the same divine essence, which is common to all three Persons. Therefore, in the Eucharist, together with the humanity and divinity of Christ (the Son of God), there are also the Father and the Holy Spirit, although for different reasons. Namely, the divine Word is present in the Eucharist by virtue of His hypostatic union with the Body and Blood of Christ, while the Father and the Holy Spirit are present by virtue of the intratrinitarian circuminsession.

From this it follows that, in every eucharistic Communion well received, a more penetrating indwelling or inhalation of the Divine Persons takes place in the soul of the just.[82] The Eucharist constitutes a true treasure for the soul that receives it worthily.

B) CONFIRMATION

The sacrament of Confirmation may be defined in the following terms: it is a sacrament instituted by our Lord Jesus Christ in which, by the imposition of hands and anointing with chrism under the prescribed formula, the fullness of the Holy Spirit is given to the baptized, together with grace and sacramental character, to strengthen Him in the Faith and to confess it boldly as a good soldier of Christ.

This broad definition contains all the essential elements that make known to us the intimate nature of this great sacrament, rightly called the sacrament of the fullness of the Holy Spirit.

The sacramental formula pronounced by the minister is as follows: "I mark you with the sign of the cross and confirm you with the chrism of salvation in the name of the Father and of the Son and of the Holy Spirit."

The Roman Catechism sets forth the effects of this sacrament as follows:

> The proper gift of Confirmation, in addition to the
> effects common to the other sacraments, is to perfect

---

[82] See STh I, q. 43 a. 6 c ad 4.

baptismal grace. Those who have been made Christians by Baptism are still like newborn children (see 1 Pet. 2:2), tender and delicate. With the sacrament of Confirmation they are strengthened against all the possible assaults of the flesh, the devil, and the world, and their souls are invigorated in the Faith to profess and confess boldly the name of our Lord Jesus Christ. Hence the name Confirmation.[83]

The sacrament of Confirmation is equivalent to a true Pentecost for each of those baptized in Christ. Like the apostles, whose weakness and cowardice during the hours of Christ's Passion became superhuman energy and strength when the fire of Pentecost descended upon them, the Christian who receives the sacrament of Confirmation feels spiritually strengthened, especially in order to proclaim and publicly defend the Faith he received in Baptism.

Fr. Philipon writes:

> The sacrament of Confirmation perpetuates in the Church all the benefits of Pentecost. The effects of Baptism are marvelously surpassed. The Holy Spirit, already in possession of the Christian soul, fills it this time with His superabundant graces, with the fullness of His gifts. The moral triumph of the virgins and martyrs is rightly attributed to Him. It is the Spirit of God who forms the souls of the saints. From this personal and mysterious presence of the Holy Spirit proceed in the soul those secret warnings, those incessant invitations, those continuous motions of the Spirit, without which no one can enlist or remain on the paths of salvation, much less

[83] Roman Catechism, II, c. 2 n. 20.

advance on the path of perfection. On the contrary, by the play and operation of the gifts of the Holy Spirit, the just person, who already lives the life of grace from His Baptism, rises to perfection. Thanks to them, the soul, docile to the least divine inspirations, advances rapidly in the life of faith, hope, charity and in the practice of all the virtues. Its spiritual life finds its full expansion and development. These gifts of the Holy Spirit work so effectively that they lead it to the highest summits of holiness.[84]

The sacrament of Confirmation imprints an indelible character or mark on the soul of the one who validly receives it (even if He received it in mortal sin, since the character is separable from the grace), by virtue of which the Christian becomes a soldier of Christ and receives the power to confess officially, ex officio, the Faith of Christ, and to receive sacred things in a more perfect way, together with the right to the actual graces that throughout His life are necessary for this confession and defense of the Faith. It is, therefore, of inestimable price and value. But precisely because of its lofty grandeur, the sacrament of Confirmation carries with it great demands and responsibilities. Here are some of the most important:

a) It requires us to build a good religious culture, as an indispensable condition for the defense of the Faith against all its enemies.

b) It forces us to despise so-called tolerance, incompatible with the ardor and courage with which the soldier of Christ must publicly proclaim his faith.

---

[84] M. M. Philipon, *Los sacramentos en la vida cristiana* (Buenos Aires: Plantín, 1950), c. 2.

c) It impels us to the apostolate in all its forms, especially in our own environment and in the special circumstances of our lives.

d) It obliges us to a continuous attention to the inner inspirations of the Holy Spirit and to an exquisite fidelity to grace. To whom much has been given, much will be asked.

CHAPTER 7

Action of the Holy Spirit in the Soul

WE HAVE JUST seen in the previous chapter how the Holy Spirit, in union with the Father and the Son, is the sweet guest of our souls—dulcis hospes animae—where He dwells as in a true living temple.

But it is quite clear and evident that the Holy Spirit does not dwell in our soul in a passive and inoperative way, but in a highly active and dynamic way, oriented to perfect it from degree to degree and to lead it, if it does not put obstacles to His divine action, to the highest summits of union with God, in which holiness consists.

As we have already indicated in the previous chapter, together with sanctifying grace, the infused virtues and the gifts of the Holy Spirit, which constitute the dynamic or operative element of our supernatural organism, are infused into our souls. Both are supernatural habits that the Holy Spirit infuses into our souls together with sanctifying grace to enable us to perform the supernatural acts proper to our condition as children of God. Without them we would not be able to perform those supernatural acts even when we are in possession of the sanctifying grace, since this, as we saw, is a supernatural, non-operative habit, which resides in the very essence of our soul in order to divinize it, but without being destined for action.[85] In order to perform supernatural acts in a manner connatural to our divine filiation, we need the corresponding operative supernatural habits, which inform the powers of our soul, elevating them to the supernatural plane and enabling them to produce those supernatural acts. These operative supernatural habits are the infused virtues and the gifts of the Holy Spirit.

Both are moved by the Holy Spirit, although in very different ways, as we will see later, in the sublime enterprise of the sanctification of the children of God.

The Infused Virtues

We will briefly explain their nature, existence, fundamental division, and in what way they act in each case under the motion of the Holy Spirit.

A) NATURE

The infused virtues are operative habits infused by God in the powers of the soul to dispose them to act supernaturally according to the dictates of reason enlightened by faith.

Its existence and necessity derive from the very nature of sanctifying grace. As a seed of God, grace is a divine seed that requires, in itself, growth and development until it reaches its perfection. But since grace is not in itself operative, even though it is radically so, as the remote principle of all our supernatural operations, it follows that, in itself, it demands and postulates some immediate principles of operation that flow from its very essence and is inseparable from it.

Otherwise, man would be elevated to the supernatural order only in the depths of his soul, but not in his powers or operative faculties, and even if God could elevate our operations to the supernatural

---

[85] Unless the violent thrust of a current grace, as we will explain shortly.

order by means of continuous actual graces, there would nevertheless be a real violence in human psychology because of the tremendous disproportion between the pure natural power and the supernatural act to be performed. Now, this violence cannot be reconciled with the gentleness of Divine Providence, which moves all beings in harmony and in accordance with their own nature.[86] The infusion of these supernatural operative principles, infused virtues, avoids this serious inconvenience, making it possible for man to tend to the supernatural end in a perfectly connatural way, gently and without violence, under the divine motion of an actual grace entirely proportioned to these infused habits.

B) EXISTENCE

The existence of the infused virtues, especially the theological virtues, which are the most important, is expressly stated in Sacred Scripture[87] and has been repeatedly proclaimed by the official Magisterium of the Church.[88]

C) DIVISION

The infused virtues are divided into two fundamental groups. The first group provides for the powers of the soul in order to the supernatural end; these are the three theological virtues (faith, hope, and charity). The second disposes the same powers in order to the means to reach that end; these are the four cardinal virtues (prudence, justice, fortitude, and temperance), with the whole cortege of their annexed or derived virtues. In all, there are more than fifty of these virtues, which St. Thomas gathers together in his marvelous

[86] See STh I–II, q. 110 a. 2.
[87] See 1 Cor. 13:13; 2 Pet. 1:5–7; Rom. 8:5–6.15; 1 Cor. 2:14; James 1:5.
[88] See Dz 410; 483; 800; 821.

Summa Theologiae.[89] With them, all the powers and energies of man are elevated to the order of grace. In each power, and in relation to each specifically distinct object, there is a supernatural habit that disposes man to act in conformity with the principle of grace and to develop supernatural life through this operation.

D) *HOW THEY ACT*

This is a very important point to determine with precision and accuracy the action of the Holy Spirit in our own sanctification.

For an infused virtue to be able to pass into an act (that is, to be able to perform the corresponding virtuous action), the prior motion of an actual grace coming from God is absolutely necessary.

Indeed, it is absolutely impossible that the purely natural effort of the soul can put the infused habits into exercise, since the natural order cannot determine the operations of the supernatural: there is an unfathomable abyss between the two, they belong to two entirely different planes, of which the supernatural surpasses and infinitely transcends the entire natural plane. Nor is it possible that these infused habits can act by themselves, because any habit can never act but by virtue of and by the action of the agent who caused it; and, in the case of infused habits, only God, who produced them, can set them in motion. Therefore, the action of God is imposed with the same absolute necessity with which, in metaphysics, the influence of a being in act is demanded, so that any power can produce its own. Speaking absolutely, God could develop and perfect sanctifying grace, infused in the very essence of our soul, on the basis only of actual graces, without infusing in the powers any supernatural

---

[89] We have explained all this at length in our *Theology of Christian Perfection*, n. 98–116, to which we refer the reader who desires further information.

operative habit.[90] On the other hand, He could not develop it without actual graces even if He endowed us with all kinds of infused operative habits, since those habits could never pass into action without the prior divine motion, which in the supernatural order is nothing other than actual grace.

Every act of any infused virtue and every act of the gifts of the Holy Spirit presupposes, therefore, a prior actual grace that has set that virtue or gift in motion.[91]

Now then: in what way does the Holy Spirit move the habit of an infused virtue? With what kind of motion? Is it the same motion with which He moves the habit of the gifts, or is it a completely different motion?

For the time being, we will tell the reader that the motion of the Holy Spirit in relation to the infused virtues is completely different from that which moves the habit of the gifts of the Holy Spirit Himself. The infused virtues are moved by the impulse of an actual grace in the human way (although of a strictly supernatural order, as is obvious, since it is a matter of moving a supernatural habit as well), while His own gifts are moved by the Holy Spirit with an actual grace in the divine or superhuman way. The result is, naturally, that the acts proceeding from the gifts of the Holy Spirit are incomparably more perfect than those proceeding from the infused virtues. In explaining the nature of the divine gift motion, we will specify in more detail this fundamental difference with the motion of the infused virtues, in order to highlight the importance and

---

[90] Although we have already said that this would be unnatural and violent. We speak now only of the absolute power of God, not of what He has actually accomplished in our souls.

[91] Of course, not every actual grace necessarily or infallibly produces an act of virtue. It can be a matter of a sufficient grace that man has wanted to resist (e.g., the sinner who feels within himself a divine inspiration, remorse, etc., and does not pay attention).

necessity of the gifts of the Holy Spirit for the full development of the Christian life in its ascent to holiness.

The Gifts of the Holy Spirit

Given the great importance of the gifts of the Holy Spirit in a work dedicated to the third Person of the Blessed Trinity, we are going to study them as extensively as the framework of our work allows.[92]

In this chapter we will limit ourselves to the study of the gifts in general, reserving for the following chapters the study of each one of them in particular.

A) God's gifts

The first great gift of God is the Holy Spirit Himself, who is the very love with which God loves Himself and loves us. The liturgy of the Church says of Him that He is the gift of the God Most High: *Altissimi donum Dei*.[93] The Holy Spirit is the first gift of God, not only insofar as He is infinite Love in the bosom of the Most Blessed Trinity, but also insofar as He is in us by mission or sending.

From this first great gift proceed all the other gifts of God, since, in the last analysis, all that God gives to creatures, both in the supernatural order and in the natural order itself, are but totally gratuitous effects of His free and infinite love.

In a broad sense, therefore, all that we have received from God are gifts of the Holy Spirit. In the proper and strict sense, certain supernatural habits infused by God into souls together with sanctifying

---

[92] The reader who desires more information can consult, among others, the magnificent work of Father I. G. Menéndez–Reigada, *Los dones del Espíritu Santo y la perfección cristiana* (Madrid: Consejo Superior de Investigaciones Científicas, 1948).

[93] Hymn *Veni, Creator* of the liturgy of Pentecost.

grace and the infused virtues, in order to their full sanctification, receive this name. In this strict sense we take them here.

B) EXISTENCE

The existence of the gifts of the Holy Spirit has its remote foundation in Sacred Scripture itself. The text of Isaiah (11:1–3) is classic:

> There shall come forth a shoot from the stump of
>   Jesse,
>   and a branch shall grow out of his roots.
>   And the Spirit of the Lord shall rest upon him,
>   the spirit of wisdom and understanding,
>   the spirit of counsel and might,
>   the spirit of knowledge and the fear of the Lord.
> And his delight shall be in the fear of the Lord.

This text is clearly messianic and properly speaks only of the Messiah.[94] Nevertheless, the saintly Fathers and the Church herself also extend it to Christ's faithful by virtue of the universal principle of the economy of grace enunciated by St. Paul when he says: "For those whom he foreknew he also predestined to be conformed to the image of his Son, in order that he might be the first-born among many brethren" (Rom. 8:29). From this it follows that whatever perfection there is in Christ, our Head, if it is communicable, is also found in His members united to Him by grace, and it is evident that the gifts of the Holy Spirit belong to the supernatural perfections that are communicable, taking into account, moreover, the need we have for them, as we shall see shortly. Therefore, since grace in necessary things is at least as prodigal as nature itself, we

---

[94] See Professors of the Pontifical University of Salamanca, *Biblia comentada, III: Libros proféticos* (Madrid: BAC, 1961), 139–143.

must rightly conclude that the seven spirits which the prophet saw resting upon Christ are also the patrimony of all those who remain united to Him by charity.

The Holy Fathers, both Greek and Latin, frequently speak of the gifts of the Holy Spirit, basing themselves, in general, on the text of Isaiah, and apply it to Christ and to every Christian in grace. Among the Greek Fathers, St. Justin, Origen, St. Cyril of Alexandria, St. Gregory Nazianzen, and Didymus the Blind of Alexandria stand out. Among the Latin Fathers, the primacy goes to St. Augustine, followed closely by St. Gregory the Great; but we also find very good things about the gifts in St. Victorinus, St. Hilary, St. Ambrose, and St. Jerome.

The Church spoke expressly of them in the Roman synod celebrated in 382 under Pope St. Damasus (see Dz 83). She repeatedly alludes to them in the liturgy of Pentecost (hymn *Veni, Creator*, in the sequence *Veni, Sancte Spiritus* of the Mass, etc.) and in the solemn administration of the sacrament of Confirmation. The immortal pontiff Leo XIII magnificently expounded the doctrine of the gifts in his encyclical *Divinum illud munus*, dedicated entirely to the Holy Spirit.

The testimony of the whole tradition, supported by a solid foundation in Sacred Scripture, leads to an absolute certainty about the existence of the gifts of the Holy Spirit in all the faithful in grace, and there is no lack of theologians of great authority who consider this existence as a truth of faith, in virtue of the ordinary and universal Magisterium of the Church.[95]

---

[95] John of St. Thomas, the best commentator of the Angelic Doctor, on the doctrine of the gifts; see *Cursus theologicus*, VI, d. 18 a. 2 n. 4 p. 583 (Vivès, Paris 1885). Among the moderns, Fr. J.A. de Aldama, *Sacrae Theologiae Summa*, III (BAC, Madrid4 1961), 726.

c) NUMBER OF GIFTS

This is a matter of secondary importance. In the Masoretic text of Isaiah, which we have collected above, only six gifts are listed, repeating at the end the gift of fear. But in the Septuagint, as in the Latin Vulgate, seven are listed, adding the gift of piety to the six of the Masoretic text. The apparent divergence between the two versions comes from the double translation of the Hebrew word *yira't* ("fear"), which can also be translated as piety.

In any case, as is well known, the Bible very frequently uses the number seven to signify an indeterminate fullness, without it having to be reduced precisely to the concrete number seven. St. Ambrose and St. Augustine insist that the number seven has here a value of fullness; that is, the whole host of desirable gifts dwelt in the Messiah.[96]

In any case, it would be foolhardy and without any objective value to improvise names other than the seven that Tradition has unanimously handed down to us. Only on the basis of these names can the theology of the gifts be seriously constructed, and this is what the Holy Fathers and theologians of all schools have done. We will also adhere to them.

d) NATURE

The gifts of the Holy Spirit are supernatural habits infused by God into the powers of the soul to receive and readily second the motions of the Holy Spirit Himself in the divine or superhuman way.

We will explain the definition word by word.

> 3. *They are supernatural habits.* In the famous text of Isaiah we are told that the gifts will rest upon

---

[96] St. Ambrose, *De Spiritu Sancto*, I, 159: PL 16, 771; St. Augustine, *De civite Dei*, 11, 31: PL 41, 344.

the Messiah, which means that they will remain in Him in a constant, habitual way. Then, similarly, they are conferred on the members of Christ also in a permanent or habitual way. Faith itself teaches us the permanent presence of the Holy Spirit in every soul in grace (1 Cor. 6:19), and the Holy Spirit is never without His gifts.

4. *Infused by God.* It is clear and evident if we take into account that we are dealing with supernatural realities, which the soul could never acquire by its own strengths, since they infinitely transcend all purely natural order.

5. *In the powers of the soul.* They are the subject in which they reside, as well as the infused virtues, whose supernatural act comes to perfect the gifts, giving them the divine or superhuman modality proper to them, as we shall see shortly.

6. *To receive and second with ease.* It is proper and characteristic of habits that they perfect the powers precisely in order to receive and second with ease the motion of the agent that moves them.

7. *The motions of the Holy Spirit Himself,* who moves them and acts directly and immediately as the motive and principal cause, unlike the infused virtues, which are moved or acted upon by man himself as the motive and principal cause, although always under the previous motion of an actual grace.

8. *To the divine or superhuman mode.* This is the main difference between the ordinary motion of

actual grace, which moves the infused virtues in
the human way, and the divine motion, which
puts into action the gifts of the Holy Spirit in
the divine or superhuman way. Let us explain
this very interesting point separately.

E) *The divine motion of the gifts*

The divine motion of the gifts is very different from the divine motion that sets in motion the infused virtues. In the divine motion of the virtues, God acts as the first principal cause, but man has full responsibility for the action as second principal cause entirely subordinate to the first. The acts of the virtues are therefore entirely our own, since they start from ourselves, from our reason and our free will, although always, of course, under the motion of God as first cause, without which no being in potency can pass to the act in the natural order or in the supernatural order.

In the case of the gifts, the divine motion that sets them in movement is very different: God acts, not as the first principal cause, as happens with the virtues, but as the only principal cause, and man ceases to be the second principal cause, passing to the category of simple instrumental cause of the effect that the Holy Spirit will produce in the soul as the only principal cause. Therefore the acts proceeding from the gifts are materially human, but formally divine, in a manner similar to the melody that an artist plucks from his harp, which is materially of the harp, but formally of the artist who handles it; this in no way diminishes the merit of the soul that instrumentally produces that divine act by docilely seconding the divine motion, since it does not act as a dead or inert instrument, like the carpenter's plane or the writer's pen, but as a living and conscious instrument that adheres with all the force of its free will to the divine motion, allowing itself to be led by it and fully seconding it.[97] The passivity of the soul under the divine motion of the gifts is only relative, that is to say, only with regard to the initiative of the act that corresponds uniquely and exclusively with the Holy Spirit. However, once it has received the divine motion, it reacts actively and associates itself very intensely with it with all the vital force of which it is capable and with all the fullness of its free will. In this way the divine initiative, the relative passivity of the soul, the vital reaction of the soul, the exercise of the free will and the supernatural merit of the action are mutually combined and complete.

This explains why, in the exercise of the infused virtues, the soul is in a fully active state. Its acts are produced in the human way, and it is fully aware that it is the soul that acts when and as it pleases (e.g., by performing an act of humility, of prayer, of obedience, etc., when it wants and how it wants). It is simply the motive and principal cause of its own acts, although always, of course, under the divine motion of ordinary actual grace, which is never lacking and is always at our disposal when we want to act virtuously, like air for breathing.

[97] St. Thomas says it expressly when answering an objection about the necessity of the gifts as habits. Here is the objection and his answer: Objection: "The gifts of the Holy Spirit perfect man insofar as he is moved by the Spirit of God. But man, moved by the Spirit of God, behaves in relation to Him as an instrument; and it is the principal agent, not the instrument, that is to be perfected by a habit. Therefore, the gifts of the Holy Spirit are not habits." Answer: "The argument would be valid in the case of an instrument whose mission is not to act, but only to be acted upon. But man is not such an instrument, but is so moved by the Holy Spirit that he too acts or is moved, inasmuch as he is endowed with free will. Therefore he needs a habit" (STh I–II, q. 68 a. 3 ad 2). St. Thomas repeats this same doctrine in many other places. See, for example, with respect to the humanity of Christ, instrument of the divine Word, who moved, however, of His own free will, seconding the action of the Word (STh III, q. 18 a. 1 ad 2).

The exercise of the gifts, as we have already said, is completely different. The Holy Spirit is the only motive and principal cause that moves the habit of the gifts, the soul passing to the category of a simple instrument, although conscious and free. The soul reacts vitally upon receiving the motion of the gifts, and in this way freedom and merit are saved under the action of the gifts, but only in order to second the divine motion, the initiative and full responsibility for which belongs entirely to the Holy Spirit Himself, who acts as the sole motive and principal cause. For this reason, the more perfect and cleaner the action of the gift is, the more the soul succeeds in seconding this divine motion with greater docility, adhering strongly to it without twisting it or diverting it with movements of human initiative, which would only hinder the sanctifying action of the Holy Spirit.

It follows from this that the soul, when it feels the action of the Holy Spirit, must repress its own human initiative and reduce its activity to docilely seconding the divine motion, remaining passive in relation to it. This passivity, it should be understood, is so only in relation to the divine agent; but, in reality, it is transformed into a very lively activity on the part of the soul, although only and exclusively to second the divine action, without altering or modifying it with human initiatives. In this sense it can and must be said that the soul also works instrumentally what is worked in it, produces what is produced in it, executes what the Holy Spirit executes in it. It is simply a matter of an activity received, of an absorption of the natural activity by a supernatural activity, of a sublimation of the powers to a divine order of operation, which has absolutely nothing to do with the sterile inaction of quietism.[98]

---

[98] "In the gifts of the Holy Spirit, the human mind does not behave as a motor, but as a mover" (STh II–II, q. 52 a. 2 ad 1).

f) NEED OF THE GIFTS OF THE HOLY SPIRIT

The gifts of the Holy Spirit are absolutely necessary for the perfection of the infused virtues—or, in other words, to reach full Christian perfection—and even for eternal salvation itself. Let us look at them separately.

First of all, the gifts of the Holy Spirit are necessary for the perfection of the infused virtues. The fundamental reason is because of the great disproportion between the infused virtues themselves and the subject wherein they reside: the human soul.

Indeed, as is well known, the infused virtues are supernatural, divine habits, and the subject in which they are received is the human soul, or, more precisely, that soul's powers or faculties.

Now then: since, according to the well-known aphorism of the theological schools, "what is received is received in the manner of the recipient," the infused virtues, when they are received in the powers of the soul, are lowered and degraded, and come to acquire our human manner (by their inevitable accommodation to the natural psychological functioning of man); they are, as it were, suffocated in that human atmosphere, which is almost unbreathable for them, and this is the reason why the infused virtues, despite being much more perfect than their corresponding acquired virtues (which are acquired by the repetition of naturally virtuous acts), do not make us act as easily as the latter, precisely because of the imperfection with which we possess the supernatural infused habits. This is very clear in a sinner who repents and confesses after a disordered life: he easily returns to his sins in spite of having received with grace all the infused virtues. This is something that does not happen with the one who, by dint of repeating virtuous acts, has come to acquire some natural or acquired virtue.

Now, it is clear and evident that if we possess the habit of the infused virtues imperfectly in the soul, the acts that proceed from it will also be imperfect, unless a superior agent comes to perfect them, and this is precisely the purpose of the gifts of the Holy Spirit. They are moved and regulated, not by human reason, like the virtues, but by the Holy Spirit Himself, who provides the infused virtues, especially the theological virtues, with the divine atmosphere they need to develop their full supernatural potential.[99]

Thus the imperfection of the infused virtues is not in themselves—they are most perfect in themselves—but in the way in which we possess them, because of their own transcendental perfection and our own human imperfection, which necessarily imprints on them the human way of simple natural reason enlightened by faith. Hence the need for the gifts of the Holy Spirit to come to the aid of the infused virtues, disposing the powers of the soul to be moved by a superior agent, the Holy Spirit Himself, who will make them act in a divine way—that is, in a way totally proportionate to the most perfect object of the infused virtues. Under the action of the gifts, the infused virtues find themselves, so to speak, in their own environment.[100]

It follows that, without the frequent and dominant action of the gifts of the Holy Spirit moving the infused virtues to the divine, they can never reach their full expansion and development, no matter how much they multiply and intensify their acts in the human way. Without the predominant regime of the gifts of the Holy Spirit, it is impossible to reach Christian perfection.[101]

---

[99] See STh I–II, q. 68 a. 2. This is the reason for the perfect uselessness of an operation of the gifts in the human way, supposing it were possible. It would solve absolutely nothing in order to the perfection of the virtues. It would continue the same imperfection of the human mode.

[100] See ibid.

[101] I. G. Menéndez–Reigada, *Necesidad de los dones del Espíritu Santo*. Speech read at the inaugural session of the academic year 1939–1940

Secondly, the gifts of the Holy Spirit are necessary, in a certain sense, even for salvation. To put it beyond any doubt, it is enough to take into account the corruption of human nature as a consequence of the Original Sin with which we all come into the world. The virtues do not reside in a healthy nature, but in one that is badly inclined to sin, and although the infused virtues, insofar as it depends on them, have sufficient strength to overcome all the temptations that oppose them, they cannot, in fact, without the help of the gifts, overcome the serious temptations that come unexpectedly and suddenly at any given moment. In these unforeseen situations, in which one falls into sin or resistance is a matter of an instant, man cannot avail himself of the slow and laborious discourse of reason, but must move quickly, as if by supernatural instinct — that is, under the motion of the gifts of the Holy Spirit, which give us precisely that kind of instinct of the divine. Without this movement of the gifts, the fall into sin would be almost certain, given the vicious inclination of human nature, wounded by original guilt.

Of course, such difficult and embarrassing situations are not frequent in the life of man. But it is enough that they may occur once in a while to conclude that, at least on those occasions, the action of the gifts becomes necessary even for eternal salvation itself.

G) The deiform mode of the gifts of the Holy Spirit
As we have explained above, the most important and fundamental characteristic of the gifts of the Holy Spirit is their action in the divine or superhuman way — that is, the divine modality that they imprint on the acts of the infused virtues when they are perfected by the gifts of the Holy Spirit. Given the exceptional importance

in the Convent of San Esteban (Salamanca, 1940).

of this doctrine in the theology of the gifts, we offer the reader Philipon's admirable explanation of these ideas:

> The most fundamental property of the gifts of the Holy Spirit is their uniform mode: their acts emanate from us, but under divine inspiration. God is their rule and their measure, their special motor.
>
> Indeed, human acts can have a triple measure:
>
> 1. A human measure, which imbues our entire moral life with the regulation of reason. This is the case of natural or acquired virtues.
>
> 2. A human–divine measure in the order of sanctifying grace, which comes to elevate greatly in its essence all our virtuous activity in order to make it participate in the life of thought, love, and action of the triune God through the Christian virtues (infused), but still leaving to man his connatural way of acting (that is, the human way), according to the deliberations of his discursive reason and the reasoned inclinations of his will. This is the common regime of the theological and moral (infused) virtues when man, divinized by the grace of adoption, performs elicit acts which, in substance, belong to the supernatural order, but whose manner of performing them remains human.
>
> 3. There is, finally, a superior regime of virtuous life, uniform not only in its substance but also in its mode, in which acts have the divine measure of the Spirit of God, who is their Motor and their

specifying Rule. This is the case of the gifts of the Holy Spirit. God is not only the efficient cause of these acts. He takes the initiative in them, inspires them, carries them out according to His divine measure, participated in in varying degrees by man, made a child of God by grace and directed by His Spirit. This deiform action shows then the way of thinking, loving, willing and acting of the Spirit of God, in the proportion possible to man, without departing from His conditions of incarnate spirit.... It is as if the man who is animated by the breath of the Spirit is caught up and sustained by the swift wings of an all-powerful eagle.

This deiform action then takes on the way of thinking, loving, willing, and acting proper to the very Spirit of God. The spiritual life of man becomes like a projection in him of the ways of the Trinity, into whose bosom he enters, in imitation of the only Son of the Father, becoming only one with Him, mystically, in the unity of the same person, transforming the Christian into "another Christ" who walks the earth, identified with all the sentiments of the incarnate Word, glorifier of the Father and Savior of men. The Christian thus advances through life, illumined in his intelligence by the clarity of the Word, with his life of love at the rhythm of the Holy Spirit, acting in all his interior and exterior conduct according to the model of the activity ad extra of the three Divine Persons in the indivisible unity of their essence. The Spirit of God becomes not only the inspirer and driving force, but also the rule, form, and life of this activity in the formless and Christian way proper to the Christian, increasingly clothed by faith, love, and practice, with all the virtues of the holiness of Christ.

In the various treatises on the gifts of the Holy Spirit, we do not insist enough on the fact that, within the concrete order of the economy of salvation, the activity of the gifts is realized in us not only in a uniform way, but also in a Christian way, which configures us to the only Son of the Father. To believe is to see everything through the eyes of Christ. We expect everything from the omnipotent and merciful Trinity, but by virtue of the merits of Christ. Our life of love for God, our Father, and for mankind, our brothers and sisters, expands into a friendship with all in the Person of Christ, and so it is with the other virtues and with the other gifts of the Holy Spirit. Our whole spiritual life develops in us, according to the expression of St. Paul, "in Christ Jesus."

The trinitarian exemplar is the supreme rule of the deiform activity of the gifts. Animated by the Holy Spirit in each of his acts, the Christian should pass through the earth in the manner of an incarnate God.[102]

The Fruits of the Holy Spirit

When the soul corresponds docilely to the interior motion of the Holy Spirit, it produces exquisite acts of virtue that can be compared to the seasoned fruits of a tree. Not all the acts that proceed from grace are rightly considered fruits, but only the most seasoned and exquisite

[102] M. M. Philipon, *The Gifts of the Holy Spirit* (Barcelona: Balmes, 1966), 149–151.

ones, which carry with them great softness and sweetness. They are simply the acts proceeding from the gifts of the Holy Spirit.[103]

They are distinguished from the gifts as the fruit is distinguished from the branch and the effect from the cause, and they are also distinguished from the evangelical Beatitudes, of which we will speak in a moment, in the degree of perfection; the latter are more perfect and finished than the fruits. Therefore all the Beatitudes are fruits, but not all the fruits are Beatitudes.[104]

The fruits are completely contrary to the works of the flesh, since the latter tend to sensible goods, which are inferior to man, while the Holy Spirit moves us to what is above us.[105]

As for the number of fruits, the Vulgate lists twelve: charity, spiritual joy, peace, patience, kindness, goodness, long-suffering, gentleness, meekness, faith, modesty, continence, and chastity (Gal. 5:22–23). But in the original Pauline text, only nine are cited: charity, joy, peace, long-suffering, gentleness, kindness, goodness, faith, meekness, temperance. This is because, as St. Thomas says so well, according to the original Pauline text with St. Augustine, the apostle did not intend to enumerate them all, but limited himself to citing a few by way of example; but in reality there are or can be many more, since they are acts, not habits, like the gifts.

The Evangelical Beatitudes

Even more perfect than the fruits are the evangelical Beatitudes. They mark the culminating point and the definitive crowning, here on earth, of the whole Christian life.

---

[103] Although not exclusively. They can also come from the virtues. According to St. Thomas, the fruits of the Holy Spirit are all those virtuous acts in which the soul finds spiritual consolation (STh I–II, q. 70 a. 2).
[104] Ibid.
[105] Ibid., a. 4.

Like the fruits, the Beatitudes are not habits, but acts.[106] Like the fruits, they come from virtues and gifts; but they are so perfect that they must be attributed to the gifts rather than to the virtues.[107] Because of the splendid rewards that accompany them, they are already in this life a foretaste of eternal Beatitude.[108]

In the Sermon on the Mount, our Lord reduces them to eight: poverty of spirit, meekness, tears, hunger and thirst for righteousness, mercy, purity of heart, peace, and persecution for righteousness' sake (Matt. 5:3–10). But we can also say that it is a symbolic number that recognizes no limits.

Here is now, in a brief schematic overview, the correspondence between the infused virtues, the gifts of the Holy Spirit, and the Gospel Beatitudes, as established by St. Thomas:[109]

VIRTUES	GIFTS	BEATITUDES
Charity	Wisdom	The peacemakers
Faith	Understanding	The pure of heart
Hope	Knowledge	Those who mourn
Prudence	Counsel	The poor in spirit
Justice	Piety	The merciful
Strength	Fortitude	Those who hunger and thirst
Temperance	Fear	The poor in spirit

[106] Ibid., q. 69 a. 1.
[107] Ibid., ad 1; q. 70 a. 2.
[108] Ibid., q. 69 a.2.
[109] Ibid., q. 68–69; II–II, q. 8 ad 3.

The above table does not include the eighth Beatitude (persecution for righteousness' sake), because, being the most perfect of all, it contains and embraces all the others in the midst of the greatest obstacles and difficulties.[110]

Let us now move on to a detailed study of each of the gifts of the Holy Spirit in particular.

---

[110] See STh I–II, q. 69 a. 3 ad 5; a. 4 ad 2.

CHAPTER 8

The Gift of the Fear of God

THE GIFTS OF the Holy Spirit are all most perfect; but there is undoubtedly a hierarchy among them that determines different degrees of excellence and perfection. This hierarchical scale begins at the base with the gift of fear and ends at the summit with the gift of wisdom, which is the most sublime and excellent of all. Let us begin, then, with the study of the gift of fear.[111]

Is It Possible for God to Be Feared?

The Angelic Doctor begins the long and magnificent question that structures his fundamental work with the gift of the fear of God, asking if God can be feared.[112]

At first glance it seems, indeed, that God cannot and should not be feared, and this by virtue of two very clear and simple arguments:

1. The object of fear is a future evil that may befall us. But from God, who is supreme goodness, no evil can come upon us. Therefore, it cannot and should not be feared.

---

[111] See our *Theology of Christian Perfection*, n. 353, 358.
[112] See STh II–II, q. 19 a.1.

2. Fear is opposed to hope, as the philosophers
   teach. But we have supreme hope in God.
   Therefore we cannot fear Him at the same time.

In spite of these difficulties, it is clear and evident that God can and should be rightly feared. It is not possible to fear God as the supreme good and future bliss of man; in this sense He is the object only of love and desire. But God is also infinitely just, who hates and punishes man's sin; and, in this sense, He can and ought to be feared, inasmuch as He can inflict evil on us in punishment for our faults.

The answer to the first difficulty is that the guilt of sin does not come from God as its author, but from ourselves, inasmuch as we turn away from Him. The punishment or penalty for sin does come from God, because it is a just penalty, and therefore a good. But the fact that God justly inflicts a penalty on us happens primarily because of our sins, as we read in the book of Wisdom: "God did not make death ... but ungodly men by their words and deeds summoned death" (Wisdom 1:13–16).

The second difficulty is removed by saying that in God we must consider justice, by which He punishes sinners, and mercy, by which He frees us. With the consideration of His justice, fear arises in us, and with the consideration of His mercy, hope invades us. In this way, under various aspects, God is the object of both hope and fear.

It should be noted, however, that there are many kinds of fear, and not all of them are perfect, or even virtuous. Let us specify this immediately.

Different Kinds of Fear

Four very different kinds of fear can be distinguished:

1. Worldly fear. It is that which does not hesitate to offend God to avoid a temporary evil (e.g., apostatizing from faith to avoid the torments of the tyrant who persecutes it). It is quite clear that this fear is not only not virtuous, but constitutes a great sin, since one prefers a created good (one's own life, in this case) to the love of the uncreated good, which is God Himself. This is why Christ says in the Gospel: "He who finds his life will lose it, and he who loses his life for my sake will find it" (Matt. 10:39). To this kind of worldly fear are reduced, to a greater or lesser degree, the sins that are committed out of human respect. St. Teresa of Jesus was far from this kind of worldly fear when she said that she preferred to be "most ungrateful to the whole world" rather than offend God in a single point.[113]

2. Servile fear. It is proper to the servant, who serves his master for fear of the punishment that, if he does not do so, could befall him. It is necessary to distinguish two modalities in this kind of fear:

   a) If the fear of punishment is the only reason for avoiding sin, it constitutes a real sin, since it cares nothing for the offense of God, but only for the fear of punishment (e.g., he who says: "I would commit sin if there were no Hell"). It is evil and sinful, because, although in fact he avoids the materiality of sin, he formally incurs it because of his affection for

---

[113] St. Teresa of Jesus, *Life*, 5, 4.

it; he would not care at all about the offense of God if it did not carry with it the penalty. In this sense it is called slavishly servile fear and is always evil and sinful.

b) If the fear of punishment is not the sole or proximate cause, but accompanies the first and principal cause (which is the fear of offending God), it is good and honest, because, after all, it rejects sin mainly because it is an offense against God and, moreover, because He can punish us if we commit it. It is the so-called pain of attrition, which the Church declares good and honest against the doctrine of Protestants and Jansenists.[114] It is also called simply servile fear.

3. Imperfect filial fear. It is that fear that avoids sin because it would separate us from God, whom we love. It is the proper fear to the son who loves his Father and does not want to be separated from Him. It is already understood that this kind of fear is very good and honest. But it is not yet entirely perfect, since it still takes into account the punishment that would befall him: separation from the Father and, therefore, from Heaven. But it is far superior to the simply servile fear, since the punishment it fears comes from the love one professes for one's Father, and not from the fear of other kinds of punishment. It is the so-called initial fear, which occupies an

[114] See Dz 818, 898, 915, 1303–1305.

intermediate place between the servile and the properly filial, as we shall see.

4. Perfect filial fear. It is that of the loving son, awaiting the Father's orders, which He will not disobey only not to displease Him, even if they did not threaten him any kind of penalty or punishment. It is the most perfect fear of the one who knows how to say in all truth: "Even if there were no Heaven, I would love you, and even if there were no Hell, I would fear you."

Now, which of these fears is a gift of the Holy Spirit?

It is evident that neither the worldly nor the servile can be. Not the worldly, because it is sinful; it fears more to lose the world than God, whom it abandons for the world. Nor the servile, because, despite not being evil in itself, it can also occur in the sinner through an actual grace that moves him to the pain of attrition for fear of the penalty. This fear is already a grace of God that moves him to repentance, but it is not yet connected with charity nor, therefore, with the gifts of the Holy Spirit.

According to St. Thomas, only perfect filial love enters into the gift of fear, because it is founded directly on charity and reverence for God as Father. But since imperfect filial fear (initial fear) does not differ substantially from perfect filial fear, imperfect filial fear also enters into the gift of fear, although only in its incipient or imperfect manifestations.

As charity grows, this initial fear is purified, losing its servile modality, which still fears the penalty, to focus solely on guilt as an offense against God.[115]

---

[115] See STh II–II, q. 19 a. 8–10.

With these notions we can now address the intimate nature of the gift of fear.

Nature

The gift of fear is one of the most complex and difficult to define with complete accuracy and theological rigor. In its most intimate and positive aspects, we could give it the following definition:

The gift of fear is a supernatural habit by which the just person, under the instinct of the Holy Spirit and dominated by a reverential feeling for the majesty of God, acquires a special docility to turn away from sin and submit himself totally to the divine will.

Let this general notion suffice for the moment. By specifying below the principal virtues to which it is related and the admirable effects produced in the soul by the action of the gift of fear, we will finish outlining the intimate nature of this admirable gift.

Its Deiform Mode

God is the supreme and exemplary cause of all the supernatural gifts that we have received from His divine liberality. But it seems that with regard to the gift of fear it is not possible to find in Him any kind of exemplarity, since in God the existence of any kind of fear is absolutely impossible.

Fr. Philipon writes:

> The divine exemplarity, which is evident in all the other gifts of the Holy Spirit, is difficult to perceive in the gift of fear.
>
> It is easy to understand that the intellectual gifts have as their prototype intelligence, knowledge, wisdom, and the counsel of God. The gift of piety is like an imitation of the glorification that God finds in

Himself, in His Word, and the gift of fortitude, as a reflection of the divine omnipotence and immutability. But how can we discover in God a model of the gift of fear?

Yes, there is one: His detachment from all evil, that is, His infinite holiness, which He communicates to men and angels, who "tremble" before Him; something of His divine purity, inaccessible to the slightest defilement and endowed with a sovereignly efficacious power against all forms of evil. The Spirit of God is a Spirit of fear, just as He is a Spirit of love, intelligence, knowledge, wisdom, counsel, fortitude and piety. In His personal action in the inmost depths of the soul, the Spirit of the Father and of the Son conveys something of the infinite abhorrence of sin that exists in God Himself, and of His will to oppose the "evil of guilt," and of His ordination of the "evil of sorrow" by His avenging justice for His greater glory and for the restoration of order in the universe.

An analogous sentiment is partaken of, in the depths of souls, under the direct influence of the Spirit of fear: first of all, an energetic detestation of sin, dictated by charity; moreover, a sentiment of reverence for the infinite greatness of Him whose sovereign goodness deserves to be the supreme end of each of our acts, without the least selfish deviation toward sin. The uniform manner of the Spirit of fear is measured by the holiness of God.[116]

[116] M. M. Philipon, *The Gifts of the Holy Spirit*, 337–38.

Related Virtues

The gifts of the Holy Spirit are intimately related to one another and to the whole set of Christian virtues, since both are inseparable from the supernatural charity, which is the form of all the virtues and gifts, the soul of them all. However, each of the gifts is especially related to some infused virtue or virtues, which it is responsible for perfecting because of its great affinity with them. The gift of fear is especially related to hope, temperance, religion, and humility. Let us look at it in detail.

1. Hope. Human beings have a natural inclination to love themselves in a disorderly way, to presume that they are something, that they have worth, and that they can achieve their blessedness. This is the sin of presumption, which is excessive and opposed to the virtue of hope. Hope will only uproot this sin by instilling in us a supernatural and vivid sense of our radical powerlessness before God. This will result in relying solely on the assisting omnipotence of God, which is precisely the formal motive of Christian hope. Without the intense action of the gift of fear, the latter will never be completely perfect.[117] Philipon writes in this regard:

   > Hope leads the human soul, conscious of its fragility and misery, to take refuge in God, whose merciful omnipotence alone can deliver it from all evil. Thus, the spirit of fear and theological hope, the sense of our

[117] See STh II–II, q. 19 a. 9 ad 1 and 2; q. 141 a. 1 ad 3.

weakness and the sense of God's omnipotence, lend each other mutual support. The gift of fear thus becomes one of the most precious aids of Christian hope. The weaker and more miserable one feels, the more one is capable of all the falls, the more one is drawn to God, as a child clings to his father's arms.[118]

2. Temperance. The gift of fear looks primarily to God, making us carefully avoid anything that might offend Him, and in this sense it perfects the virtue of hope, as we have already said. But secondarily it can look to anything else from which man turns away in order to avoid offending God, and in this sense it corresponds to the gift of fear to correct the most disordered tendency that man experiences—that of carnal pleasures—by repressing it through divine fear, aiding and strengthening the virtue of temperance, which is responsible for moderating that disordered tendency. Without the reinforcement of the gift of fear, the virtue of temperance would be powerless to overcome always and everywhere the impetus of the disordered passions.[119]

3. Religion. As is well known, religion is the virtue in charge of regulating the worship due to the majesty of God. When this virtue is perfected by the gift of fear, it reaches its maximum exponent and full perfection. The worship of the Divinity

[118] M. M. Philipon, *The Gifts of the Holy Spirit*, 339.
[119] See STh II–II, q. 141 a. 3 ad 3.

is then filled with that reverential fear that the angels themselves experience before the majesty of God, *tremunt potestates*; with that holy fear that is translated into profound adoration before the infinite perfection of God: "Holy, holy, holy is the Lord of hosts" (Isa. 6:3). The supreme model of this reverence before the greatness and majesty of God is Christ Himself. If it were given to us to contemplate the humanity of Jesus, we would see it in awe before the Word of God, to whom it was united hypostatically, that is, forming a single Divine Person with Him. This is the reverence that the Holy Spirit puts in our souls through the gift of fear. He takes care to foster it in us, moderating it and merging it with the gift of piety, which puts in our souls a feeling of love and filial tenderness, the fruit of our divine adoption, which allows us to call God our Father.

4. Humility. The infinite contrast between the greatness and holiness of God and our incredible smallness and misery is the foundation and root of Christian humility; but only the gift of fear, acting intensely in the soul, brings humility to the sublime perfection that we admire in the saints. Let us listen to a contemporary theologian explaining this doctrine:

> Man, above all, loves his greatness, to ex-
> pand and widen himself more than what
> corresponds to him, which constitutes
> pride, arrogance; but humility reduces him

to his due limits so that he does not pretend to be more than what he is according
to the rule of reason, and upon this comes
to act the gift of fear, submerging the soul
in the abyss of its nothingness before the
all of God, in the depths of its misery before the infinite justice and divine majesty,
and so, penetrated by this gift, since the
soul is nothing before God and has nothing on its side but its misery and sin, it
does not seek for itself any greatness or
glory outside of God, nor does it judge itself worthy of anything other than contempt and punishment. Only in this way
can humility reach its perfection: and such
was the humility we see in the saints, with
absolute self-contempt.[120]

Alongside these four fundamental virtues, the gift of fear also makes
its influence felt on several others, related in some way to them.

There is no virtue which, through any theological or cardinal
virtue, fails to receive the influence of some gift, and so, through
temperance, the gift of fear acts on chastity, bringing it to the
most exquisite delicacy; on meekness, totally repressing disordered anger; on modesty, suppressing absolutely any interior
or exterior disordered movement; and it combats the passions
which, together with vainglory, are the daughters of pride: boast-
ing, presumption, hypocrisy, pertinacity, discord, angry retort,
and disobedience.[121]

---

[120] I. G. Menéndez–Reigada, *Los dones del Espíritu Santo y la perfección cristiana*, 579–580; see STh II–II, q. 19 a. 9 ad 4.
[121] See STh II–II, q. 132 a. 5.

Effects

The sanctifying effects produced in souls by the action of the gift of fear are invaluable, even though it is the last and least perfect of all.[122] Here are the principal ones:

First, a lively feeling of the greatness and majesty of God. This feeling immerses souls in a profound adoration, full of reverence and humility. It is the most characteristic effect of the gift of fear, which follows from its very definition. The soul subjected to its action is transported with irresistible force before the greatness and majesty of God, which makes the angels themselves tremble. Before that infinite majesty it feels nothing and less than nothing, since it is a sinful nothing; it is seized by such a strong and penetrating feeling of reverence, submission, and obeisance, that it would like to be undone and suffer a thousand deaths for God.

It is then that humility reaches its peak. Souls feel an immense desire to "suffer and be despised by God" (to use the words of St. John of the Cross). It does not occur to them to have the slightest thought of vanity or presumption. They see so clearly their misery, that when they praise themselves, it seems to them that they are being mocked (to paraphrase the Curé d'Ars). St. Dominic de Guzman used to kneel at the entrance of the towns, asking God not to punish that town where such a great sinner was going to enter. At this point, there is an infallible procedure to attract the sympathy and friendship of these servants of God: to insult them and fill them with insults (per St. Teresa of Jesus).

This respect and reverence for the majesty of God is also manifested in all things that in any way relate to Him. The church or oratory, the priest, the sacred vessels, the images of the saints—everything is looked upon and treated with the greatest respect and

[122] Ibid., q. 19 a. 9.

veneration. The gift of piety also produces similar effects, but from another point of view, as we shall see later on.

This is the aspect of the gift of fear that will continue eternally in Heaven.[123] There, given the absolute impeccability of the blessed, fear of the offense of God will not be possible; but reverence and respect before the infinite greatness and majesty of God, which will fill the intelligence and heart of the saints with awe, will remain eternally, perfected and purified.

Second, a great horror of sin and a very lively contrition for having committed it. With its faith enlightened by the radiance of the gifts of understanding and knowledge, and its hope subjected to the action of the gift of fear, which confronts it directly with the divine majesty, the soul understands as never before the infinite malice that is contained in any offense against God, no matter how insignificant it may seem. The Holy Spirit, who wants to purify the soul more and more for the divine union, subjects it to the gift of fear, which makes it experience a kind of foretaste of the inexorable rigor with which divine justice, offended by sin, will punish it in the next life if it does not perform due penance in this one. The poor soul feels moral anguish, which reaches its maximum intensity in the horrendous night of the spirit, before reaching the supreme summit of Christian perfection. It seems to him that he is irretrievably condemned and that he has nothing more to hope for. In fact, it is then that hope reaches an incredible degree of heroism, for the soul comes to hope against all hope, like Abraham (Rom. 4:18), and to utter the sublime cry of Job: "Behold, he will slay me; I have no hope; yet I will defend my ways to his face" (Job 13:15).

The horror that these souls experience before sin is so great that St. Aloysius Gonzaga fell fainting at the feet of his confessor when

[123] Ibid., a. 11.

he accused himself of two very minor venial faults. St. Alphonsus Liguori experienced a similar phenomenon when he heard himself utter a blasphemy. St. Teresa of Jesus writes that "there could be no more painful death for me than to think if I had offended God,"[124] and St. Louis Beltran was seized by an impressive trembling at the thought of the possibility of condemning himself, thus eternally losing God. His repentance for the slightest fault is very lively. From the Spirit comes the yearning for reparation, the thirst for immolation, the irresistible tendency to crucify themselves in a thousand ways that these souls continually experience. They are not mad. It is a natural consequence of the motions of the Holy Spirit through the gift of fear.

Third, an extreme vigilance to avoid the least occasion to offend God. The previous effect is a logical consequence. These souls fear nothing so much as the least offense against God. They have seen clearly, in the contemplative light of the gifts of the Holy Spirit, that in reality this is the only evil on earth; the others do not deserve the name of such. How far these souls are from voluntarily meddling with occasions of sin! There is no person so apprehensive who would flee with such speed and alacrity from a sick man as these souls from the least shadow or danger of offending God. This extreme vigilance and constant attention make these souls live, under the special motion of the Holy Spirit, with such great purity of conscience, that sometimes it makes it impossible, for lack of matter, to receive sacramental absolution, unless they submit to it some fault of the past life, on which sorrow and repentance again fall.

Fourth, perfect detachment from everything created. The gift of knowledge, as we shall see, produces this same effect, but from

[124] *Life*, 34, 10.

another point of view. As we have already said, the gifts are mutually connected with each other and with charity, and they intertwine and influence one another.[125]

It is perfectly understandable. The soul that through the gift of fear has glimpsed the greatness and majesty of God must necessarily consider all created greatness as garbage and dung (Phil 3:8). Honors, riches, power, dignities—he considers everything as less than straw, as something unworthy of deserving a minute's attention. Remember the effect that produced in St. Teresa the jewels that her friend Luisa de la Cerda showed her in Toledo: it did not fit in her head that people can feel appreciation for a few crystals that shine a little more than the ordinary:

> I was laughing to myself and feeling sorry to see what men esteem, remembering what the Lord has in store for us, and I thought how impossible it would be for me, even if I wanted to try to do it myself, to have any regard for those things if the Lord did not take away the memory of higher things.[126]

Beatitudes and the Fruits Derived from It

According to the Angelic Doctor, two Gospel Beatitudes are related to the gift of fear: the first, "Blessed are the poor in spirit, for theirs is the kingdom of heaven" (Matt. 5:3), and the second, "Blessed are those who mourn, for they shall be comforted" (Matt. 5:4).

The first corresponds directly to the gift of fear, since, by virtue of the filial reverence which it makes us feel before God, it impels us not to seek our puffed-up spirit, nor our own exaltation (pride),

[125] See STh I–II, q. 68 a. 5.
[126] *Life*, 38, 4.

nor exterior goods (honors and riches). The poverty of spirit is understood as the annihilation of the arrogant and puffed-up spirit, as St. Augustine says, or as the detachment from all temporal things by the instinct of the Holy Spirit. All of this belongs to poverty of spirit, whether it is understood as the annihilation of the proud and puffed-up spirit, as St. Augustine says, or the detachment from all temporal things by the instinct of the Holy Spirit, as St. Ambrose and St. Jerome say.[127]

Indirectly, the gift of fear is also related to the Beatitude concerning those who weep.[128] For from the knowledge of the divine excellence and of our littleness and misery follows the contempt of all earthly things and the renunciation of carnal delectations, with weeping and sorrow for past misdeeds.

Hence it is clear that the gift of fear restrains all the passions, both those of the irascible appetite and those of the concupiscible. For, by reverential fear of the divine majesty offended by sin, it restrains the impetus of the irascible (hope, despair, audacity, fear, and anger) and governs and moderates that of the concupiscible (love, hatred, desire, aversion, joy, and sadness). It is, therefore, a gift of inestimable value, although it occupies hierarchically the last place among them all.

Of the so-called fruits of the Holy Spirit (see Gal 5:22–23), the gift of fear includes modesty, which is a consequence of man's reverence for the divine majesty, as well as continence and chastity, which follow from the moderation and channeling of the concupiscible passions, the proper effect of the gift of fear.[129]

[127] See STh II–II, q. 19 a. 12.
[128] Ibid., ad 2.
[129] Ibid., ad 4.

Opposing Vices

Pride, according to St. Gregory, is more strongly opposed to the gift of fear than the virtue of humility.[130] For the gift of fear, as we have seen, is fixed first of all on the eminence and majesty of God, before which man, by the instinct of the Holy Spirit, feels his own nothingness and vileness. Humility also fixes itself preferentially on the greatness of God, in contrast with its own nothingness, but in the light of simple reason enlightened by faith and, for the same reason, with a human and imperfect modality.[131] Hence it is evident that the gift of fear excludes pride in a higher way than the virtue of humility. Fear excludes even the root and the principle of pride, as St. Thomas says.[132] Therefore, pride is opposed to the gift of fear in a deeper and more radical way than to the virtue of humility.

The vice of presumption, which injures divine justice by relying excessively and disorderly on mercy, is also indirectly opposed to the gift of fear. In this sense, St. Thomas says that presumption is opposed to the gift of fear by reason of the matter — that is, insofar as it despises something divine, of which it is proper to reverence God.[133]

Means of Fostering This Gift

As we have already explained, the gifts of the Holy Spirit can only be exercised by the infused virtues, which we can act upon ourselves under the influence of a simple present grace, which God always places at our disposal, like air to breathe. However, we can and must ask the Holy Spirit to enact His gifts in us, while at the same

---

[130] St. Gregory, *Morales*, c. 32: PL 75, 547AB; see STh I–II, q. 68 a. 6 ad 2.
[131] See STh I–II, q. 161 a. 1–2.
[132] Ibid., q. 19 a. 9 ad 4; q. 161 a. 2 ad 3.
[133] Ibid., q. 130 a. 2 ad 1; q. 21 a. 3.

time doing all we can on our part to dispose ourselves to receive the divine movement that will set the gifts in motion.

Apart from the general means of attracting the merciful gaze of the Holy Spirit (deep recollection, purity of heart, exquisite fidelity to grace, frequent invocation of the divine Spirit, and so on), here are some means more closely related to the gift of fear:

1. Meditate frequently on the infinite greatness and majesty of God. We will never, by far, be able to acquire with our poor discursive efforts the lively and penetrating contemplative knowledge that the gifts of the Holy Spirit provide.[134] But we can do something by reflecting on the power and majesty of God, who brought all things out of nothing by the mere power of His will (Genesis 1:1), who calls the stars by name and they immediately come trembling with awe (Bar. 3:33–36), who is more awesome than the raging sea (Ps. 92:4), who will come on the clouds of Heaven with great power and majesty to judge the living and the dead (Luke 21:27), and before whom the angelic principalities and powers will eternally tremble with awe.

2. Get used to treating God with filial trust, full of reverence and respect. Let us never forget that God is our Father, but simultaneously He is the God of tremendous greatness and majesty. Often pious souls forget the latter and allow themselves

---

[134] "To meditate on Hell, for example, is to see a painted lion; to contemplate Hell is to see a living lion": L. Lallemant, *La doctrina espiritual* (Bilbao: Desclée, 1960) princ. 7 c. 4 a. 5. It is well known that contemplation is the effect of the intellective gifts of the Holy Spirit.

excessive familiarity in their dealings with God, full of irreverent daring. It is certainly incredible to what extent the Lord carries His trust and familiarity with the souls who are pleasing to Him, but He must take the initiative. In the meantime, the soul must remain in a reverent and submissive attitude, which is far from being detrimental to the sweet confidence and intimacy proper to adopted children.

3. Meditate frequently on the infinite malice of sin and conceive a great horror of it. The motives of love are of themselves more powerful and efficacious than those of fear in avoiding sin as an offense against God. But these also contribute powerfully to restrain us from crime. The memory of the terrible punishments that God has prepared for those who definitely despise His laws would be quite enough to make us flee from sin if we would meditate on it with seriousness and prudent reflection. "It is a fearful thing," says St. Paul, "to fall into the hands of the living God." (Heb. 10:31). We should think of this often, especially when temptation comes to place before us the blandishments of the world or of the flesh. We must try to conceive such a great horror of sin that we are ready and willing to lose all things and even our own life rather than commit it. To this end, we will be greatly helped by fleeing from dangerous occasions, which would bring us closer to sin; by fidelity to the daily examination of conscience, in order to prevent voluntary faults and to mourn for those that have escaped us; and, above all, by the

consideration of Jesus Christ crucified, the propitiatory victim for our crimes and sins.

4. Pay special attention to meekness and humility in dealing with one's neighbor. He who is clearly aware that the God of infinite majesty has mercifully forgiven him ten thousand talents, how will he dare to demand with haughtiness and contempt the hundred denarii that a fellow-servant, his brother, may owe him? (Matt. 18:23–35) We must cordially forgive offenses, treat everyone with exquisite delicateness, with profound humility and submission, considering them all as better than ourselves (at least inasmuch as they probably would not have resisted grace as much as we do if they had received the gifts that God has given us with such abundance and prodigality). He who has committed any mortal sin in His life can never humble himself enough: he is "ransomed from Hell," and there is no place so low outside of it that is not too high and lofty for him who deserved an eternal place at Satan's feet.

5. Frequently ask the Holy Spirit for the reverential fear of God. After all, every perfect disposition is a gift of God, which we can attain only through humble and persevering prayer. The liturgy is full of sublime formulas: "My flesh trembles for fear of thee, and I am afraid of thy judgments" (Ps. 119:120); "Confirm to thy servant thy promise, which is for those who fear thee" (Ps. 119:38), and so on. These and other similar formulas should flow frequently from our hearts and lips, convinced that "the fear of

the Lord is the beginning of wisdom" (Prov. 9:10) and that we must work out our salvation "with fear and trembling" (Phil. 2:12), following the advice given to us by the Holy Spirit Himself through the psalmist: "Serve the Lord with fear, with trembling" (Ps. 2:11).

CHAPTER 9

The Gift of Fortitude

IN THE ASCENDING scale of the gifts of the Holy Spirit, the gift of fortitude occupies second place, primarily responsible for perfecting the infused virtue of the same name.

Let us study it with the care and attention that its great importance in the spiritual life deserves.[135]

Nature

The gift of fortitude is a supernatural habit that strengthens the soul to practice, by instinct of the Holy Spirit, all kinds of heroic virtues with invincible confidence in overcoming the greatest dangers or difficulties that may arise.

Let us explain the definition a little, word for word.

1. It is a supernatural habit, like the other infused gifts and virtues.

2. It strengthens the soul. Its mission is precisely to elevate its forces to the plane of the divine, as we shall see shortly.

[135] See our *Theology of Christian Perfection*, n. 442–47.

3. To practice by instinct of the Holy Spirit. This is proper and specific to the gifts. Under its action, the soul does not discourse or reason; it acts by an interior impulse, like an instinct, which proceeds directly or immediately from the Holy Spirit Himself, who sets His gifts in motion.

4. All kinds of heroic virtues. Although the virtue that the gift of fortitude comes to perfect and on which it falls directly is that of the same name, nevertheless, its influence reaches all the other virtues, whose practice to a heroic degree presupposes a truly extraordinary fortitude of soul, which could not be provided by virtue alone left to itself.[136] This is why the gift of fortitude, which has to embrace so many and such diverse acts of virtue, needs, in turn, to be governed by the gift of counsel.[137] Fr. Lallemant warns:

> This gift is a habitual disposition which the Holy Spirit puts in the soul and body to do and suffer extraordinary things, to undertake the most difficult actions, to expose oneself to the most fearful harms, to overcome the rudest labors, to endure the most horrendous sorrows, and this constantly and in a heroic manner.[138]

---

[136] "The higher a power is," writes St. Thomas, "the more it extends to a greater number of things ... and, for the same reason, the gift of fortitude extends to all the difficulties that can arise in human things.... The principal act of the gift of fortitude is to endure all difficulties, whether in the passions or in operations": In III *Sent.* d. 34 q. 3 a. 1.

[137] See STh II–II, q. 139 a. 1 ad 3.

[138] L. Lallemant, *The Spiritual Doctrine*, princ. 4 c. 4 a. 6.

5. With invincible confidence. This is one of the
   clearest notes of differentiation between virtue
   and the gift of fortitude. Virtue, says St. Thomas,
   has as its mission the strengthening of the soul to
   endure any difficulty or danger; but to give the
   soul the invincible confidence that it will overcome difficulties belongs, in fact, to the gift of
   fortitude.[139] In expounding this concrete point,
   Fr. Arrighini rightly notes:

> In spite of the similarity of the definition, the
> gift of fortitude must not be confused with
> the cardinal virtue of the same name. For al-
> though both presuppose a certain firmness
> and energy of spirit, the virtue of fortitude has
> its limits in human power, which it can never
> surpass; but the gift of the same name, on the
> other hand, is based on divine power, accord-
> ing to the expression of the prophet: "By my
> God I can leap over a wall" (Ps. 18:30), that
> is, I will break through all the obstacles that
> may arise in order to reach the ultimate goal.
>
> Secondarily, if the cardinal virtue of fortitude
> provides sufficient courage to face such obsta-
> cles in general, it does not, however, instill the
> confidence to face and overcome them all, as
> does the analogous gift of the Holy Spirit.
>
> Moreover, the virtue of fortitude, precisely be-
> cause it is limited by human power, does not
> extend equally to all kinds of difficulties; and

[139] See STh II–II, q. 139 a. 1 ad 1.

so there is the case of one who easily over-
comes the temptations of pride, but not so
much those of the flesh; or who avoids certain
kinds of dangers, but not others, and so forth.
The gift of fortitude, on the other hand, being
completely based on divine omnipotence, extends to everything, is sufficient for everything
and makes us exclaim with Job: "Set me, O
my God, near you, and let him who will,
come and assail me" (Job 17:3).

Finally, the virtue of fortitude does not always achieve its object, since it is not proper
to man to overcome all dangers and win in
all struggles; but God can very well do this,
and since the gift of fortitude infuses us precisely with divine power, man can with it
overcome every danger and enemy with agil-
ity, fight and win in every battle, and repeat
with the apostle: "I can do all things in him
who strengthens me" (Phil. 4:13).

For all these reasons it is easy to understand
that the gift of fortitude is far superior to the
virtue of the same name.

The former brings its energy from grace to
the extent that human power allows; the latter to the extent that is necessary to fight and
conquer. The former always works in the
human way; the latter in the divine way. Fortitude, as a virtue, is always linked to the re-
straint and judgment of Christian prudence;
the gift, on the other hand, leads to

resolutions which, without it, would seem to
be presumptions, rashness, exaggerations. It
is precisely to this that we owe the criticisms
and false judgments that even sensible and
believing men allow themselves to make
about certain heroic deeds of our saints.
They judge them according to prudence,
even Christian prudence if you will; they
judge them in the way they themselves might
act. But they do not think that in the saints
there is another much higher and more powerful engine that can make them run and
jump to unreachable heights with their poor
legs. It is necessary to take this very much
into account in order to judge correctly these
apparent follies of the saints.[140]

There is, in fact, a great difference between the possibilities of acquired virtue, infused virtue, and the gift of fortitude, although all
three bear the same name, and so:

1. Natural or acquired fortitude strengthens the
   soul to endure the greatest labors and to expose
   oneself to the greatest dangers, as we see in many
   pagan heroes; but not without a certain trembling and anxiety, born of the clear perception of
   the weakness of one's own strength, the only
   strength one can count on.

2. Infused fortitude is certainly based on divine
   help, which is in itself omnipotent and

---

[140] A. Arrighini, *Il Dio ignoto*, 334–36.

invincible, but its exercise is conducted in the human way—that is, according to the rule of reason enlightened by faith, which does not completely remove fear and trembling from the soul.

3. The gift of fortitude, on the other hand, makes the soul bear the greatest evils and expose itself to the most unprecedented dangers with great confidence and security, because it is moved by the Holy Spirit Himself, not by the dictates of simple prudence but by the gift of counsel, whether it be for entirely natural or divine reasons.[141]

Importance and Necessity

The gift of fortitude is absolutely necessary for the perfection of the cardinal virtue of the same name, for the perfection of all the infused virtues and, at times, even for the simple permanence in the state of grace. Let us look at it in particular.

1. For the perfection of the cardinal virtue of fortitude. The fundamental reason is that which we have already indicated above. Although the virtue of fortitude tends of itself to strengthen the soul against all kinds of difficulties and dangers, it does not fully achieve this as long as it remains subject to the rule of reason enlightened by faith (the human way). It is necessary that the gift of fortitude uproot all motives of

---

[141] See John of St. Thomas, *Cursus theologicus*, I–II d. 18 a. 6.

fear or indecision by submitting it to the direct
and immediate movement of the Holy Spirit
(divine mode), which gives it unshakable confidence and security.[142] Here is how Fr. Arrighini
expounds this doctrine:

> The first effect of the gift of fortitude is to
> complete the cardinal virtue of the same
> name and take it to where it alone, with the
> human energies it can dispose of, would
> never reach. It is necessary to agree that to
> such energies the gift of fortitude adds other
> supernatural energies that invigorate the will,
> inflame the sentiment, excite the imagination
> and all the other nobler faculties of the soul
> to dispose them serenely to the greatest risks.
> Experience demonstrates, moreover, that
> many times the supernatural vigor of such a
> gift also extends to the body, communicating
> to it a resistance and energy far superior to
> ordinary vigor, and which cannot fail to fill
> with astonishment those who do not know
> the divine source from which it springs.
>
> By virtue of this source — that is, of the forti-
> tude infused by the Holy Spirit, especially in
> the sacrament of Confirmation — the world
> has been able to contemplate, throughout
> twenty centuries, incredible marvels. It has
> seen millions of souls, rich and poor, learned
> and ignorant, old and young, living in all

[142] See STh II–II, q. 139 a. 1 ad 1.

states and conditions, in all latitudes, in the midst of all dangers, strong, full of courage, constant in the execution of their Christian duties, in overcoming the temptations of the world, of the devil, and of the flesh, in fighting and overcoming all kinds of enemies and dangers. The Holy Spirit Himself gives His own testimony through the mouth of St. Paul: "Who through faith conquered kingdoms, enforced justice, received promises, stopped the mouths of lions, quenched raging fire, escaped the edge of the sword, won strength out of weakness, became mighty in war, put foreign armies to flight" (Heb. 11:33–34).

Thus we know what so many Christians have done with the gift of fortitude. Let us now see what they have endured and suffered: "Women received their dead by resurrection. Some were tortured, refusing to accept release, that they might rise again to a better life. Others suffered mocking and scourging, and even chains and imprisonment. They were stoned, they were sawn in two, they were killed with the sword; they went about in skins of sheep and goats, destitute, afflicted, ill-treated — of whom the world was not worthy — wandering over deserts and mountains, and in dens and caves of the earth" (Heb. 11:35–38). Behold what the whole world has been able to see and admire.[143]

[143] A. Arrighini, *Il Dio ignoto*, 336–38.

2. For the perfection of the other infused virtues. A virtue can be called perfect only when its act springs from the soul with energy, promptness, and unwavering perseverance. Now, this continuous heroism, never to be denied, is frankly supernatural, and can only be satisfactorily explained by the superhuman action of the gifts of the Holy Spirit—particularly, in this sense, the gift of fortitude.

3. To remain in a state of grace. There are occasions in which the dilemma presents itself inexorably: heroism or mortal sin, one or the other. In these cases, much more frequent than one might think, the simple virtue of fortitude is not enough. Precisely because of the violent, sudden, and unexpected nature of the temptation (the acceptance or rejection of which, moreover, happens in a matter of seconds), the slow and discursive manner of the virtues of prudence and fortitude is not enough; the rapid intervention of the gifts of counsel and fortitude is necessary. As we have already seen, the Angelic Doctor bases himself on this argument to proclaim the necessity of the gifts, even for eternal salvation.[144]

Fr. Lallemant writes:

> This gift is extremely necessary on certain occasions in which one feels himself to be combated by pressing temptations, which, if one wishes to resist, one must

[144] See STh I–II, q. 68 a. 2.

resolve to lose one's goods, one's honor, or one's life. In these cases, the Holy Spirit helps powerfully with His counsel and strength the faithful soul who, distrustful of itself and convinced of its weakness and nothingness, implores His help and places all its trust in Him.

In these times, ordinary graces are not enough; we need extraordinary lights and help. For this reason, the prophet Isaiah enumerates together the gifts of counsel and of strength; the first, to enlighten the spirit, and the other, to strengthen the heart.[145]

Insisting on these reasons and specifying them in relation to the three main enemies of the soul, another excellent author writes:

From all that we have just said, it is easy to understand that the gift of fortitude is not necessary only for heroes, martyrs, or for the accomplishment of extraordinary undertakings; no less than the other gifts of the Holy Spirit, it is sometimes necessary indiscriminately to all men to achieve their eternal salvation and, therefore, to live in a Christian way and to fight and win in this great battle that is the life of man on earth, as the Holy Spirit Himself warns us through the mouth of Job: "Has not man a hard service upon earth, and are not his days like the days of a hireling?" (Job 7:1)

Experience proves it. It is a continuous battle against everything and everyone. Against our own corrupt nature, since all of us—not excluding the apostle himself, who was caught up to the third Heaven—feel in our members another law that is repugnant to the law of God and draws us into sin

[145] L. Lallemant, *The Spiritual Doctrine*, princ. 4 c. 4 a. 6.

(Rom. 7:23), which must be resisted if we do not want to reach the desolate conclusion of that pagan poet who said: "I see the best and approve of it, but I do the worst" (Ovid, *Metamorphoses*, l.7, v. 20–21).

a) Battle against our passions. Like a barking dog, says Father Lacordaire, they lurk in the depths of our hearts, ready to bark and bite at the slightest opportunity. A trifle is enough: the sight of a person, the reading of a page of a novel or a newspaper, a word, a smile, a gesture, to awaken them suddenly; but how many struggles and fatigues to restrain them and submit them to right reason!

b) Battle against the world. Against its corrupt and corrupting morals, its bad company, its innumerable seductions, its scandalous fashions, its pleasures, its impure parties. It is impossible, Plato himself used to say, even though he was a pagan, to live honestly for a long time in the midst of the world; an angel himself would eventually fall without special help from the Holy Spirit.

c) Battle against the devil. He is the worst and most terrible enemy. We do not see him, we do not feel him, we do not know where he comes from and where he is going. But it is certain, as St. Peter says, that he is found everywhere and is stirring around us "like a roaring lion, seeking some one to devour" (1 Pet. 5:8). If Christ our Lord Himself was tempted three times by the devil, who can remain safe and calm?

We all have to fight continuously—against ourselves, against our passions, against the world, against the devil—and there are still many other enemies: the illnesses that threaten our health, misfortunes, the never-ending troubles, worries, annoyances. Job rightly said that the life of man on earth is a continuous and endless struggle.

Now, how can man alone, even if he is helped by the Christian virtue of fortitude, which uses only his human energies, not even so much as overcome, but merely confront so many and so powerful enemies? It is easy to understand that he will need something else, a divine help, a strictly superhuman fortitude, which is precisely that which the gift of the divine Spirit can infuse into his soul and his very members."[146]

Effects

The effects that the gift of fortitude produces in the soul are admirable. Here are the main ones:

First, it provides the soul with unwavering energy in the practice of virtue. This is an inevitable consequence of the superhuman way in which the virtue of fortitude is practiced through the gift. The soul knows no faintness or weakness in the exercise of virtue. It naturally feels the weight of the day and heat, but with superhuman energy it continues onward, undaunted in spite of all the difficulties.

Perhaps no one has known how to expose with such force and energy the dispositions of these souls as St. Teresa of Jesus did when she wrote these words:

[146] A. Arrighini, *Il Dio ignoto*, 338–40.

I say that this is very important, and the whole of it:
a great and very determined determination not to stop
until reaching it (perfection), come what may, happen
what may happen, work out what may work out,
murmur whoever murmurs, even if you arrive there,
even if you die on the way or have no heart for the
work left in it, even if the world sinks.[147]

This is frankly superhuman and a very clear effect of the gift of
fortitude. Meynard summarizes very well the main effects of this
superhuman energy as follows:

The effects of the gift of fortitude are interior and exterior. The interior is a vast field open to all generosities
and sacrifices, often reaching heroism; they are inces-
sant and victorious struggles against the solicitations of
Satan, against love and self-seeking, against impatience.
Outwardly, they are new and magnificent triumphs
obtained by the Holy Spirit against error and vice; and
also our poor body, participating in the effects of a truly
divine fortitude and giving itself with ardor, supernaturally aided, to the practices of mortification or suffering
without fainting the cruelest pains. The gift of fortitude
is, then, truly the beginning and the source of great
things undertaken or suffered by God.[148]

Second, it completely destroys lukewarmness in the service of God. It
is a natural consequence of this superhuman energy. Lukewarmness,
the true tuberculosis of the soul, which has completely paralyzed so

---

[147] St. Teresa of Jesus, *The Way of Perfection*, 21, 2.
[148] A.–M. Meynard, *Traité de la vie intérieure*, I (Paris: Librairie Caholique Bellet, 1885), 24.

many people on the road to perfection, is almost always due to a lack of energy and fortitude in the practice of virtue. It is too hard for them to overcome so many things and to keep up their spirit day after day in the monotony of the exact fulfillment of duty, even in its smallest details. Most souls faint from weariness and give up the struggle, surrendering themselves to a routine, mechanical life without horizons, when they do not turn their backs completely and abandon the path of virtue. Only the gift of fortitude, strengthening to a superhuman degree the strength of the soul, is a proportionate and effective remedy to destroy absolutely and completely lukewarmness in the service of God.

Third, it makes the soul fearless and courageous in the face of all kinds of dangers or enemies. This is another of the great purposes or effects of the gift of fortitude, which appears with impressive characters in the lives of the saints. The apostles who, cowardly and fearful, abandon their Master on the night of Holy Thursday, appear before the people on the morning of Pentecost with superhuman fortitude and courage. They fear no one. They do not take into account at all the prohibition imposed by the leaders of the Synagogue against preaching in the name of Jesus, because they say, "We must obey God rather than men" (Acts 5:29). They were beaten and reviled, and they left the council "rejoicing that they were counted worthy to suffer dishonor for the name" (Acts 5:41). All confessed their Master with martyrdom, and Peter, who was so cowed by the crowd that he did not hesitate to deny his Master, died with incredible fortitude, crucified upside down, confessing the Master whom he once denied. All this was perfectly superhuman, the effect of the gift of fortitude that the apostles received, with immense fullness, on the morning of Pentecost.

After them there are countless examples in the lives of the saints. One can hardly imagine the difficulties and dangers that St. Louis, King of France, had to overcome in order to lead the Crusade; St.

Catherine of Siena to bring the pope back to Rome; St. Teresa to reform an entire religious order; St. Joan of Arc to fight with arms against the enemies of God and her country, and so on. There were real mountains of dangers and difficulties that came their way, but nothing was able to stop them. Putting their trust only in God, they went forward with superhuman energy until they girded their foreheads with the laurel of victory. It was simply a marvelous effect of the gift of fortitude that dominated their spirits.

Fourth, it makes one bear the greatest pains with joy and happiness. Resignation, although a very praiseworthy virtue, is nevertheless imperfect. The saints properly do not know it. They are not resigned in the face of pain: they go out joyfully to meet it, and sometimes this madness of the cross manifests itself in incredible penances and macerations (Mary Magdalene, Margaret of Cortona, Henry Suson, Peter of Alcantara), and sometimes in heroic patience, with which they endure, with their bodies broken, but their souls radiant with joy, the greatest sufferings, illnesses, and pains. St. Thérèse of the Child Jesus used to say: "I have come to the point of not being able to suffer, because every suffering is sweet to me."[149] A truly superhuman language of heroism, which proceeds directly and immediately from the very intense action of the gift of fortitude! The examples are innumerable in the lives of the saints.

Finally, it provides the soul with the "heroism of the small," in addition to the heroism of the great. No greater fortitude is needed to suffer martyrdom all at once than to endure without the slightest faintness that martyrdom by pinpricks which constitutes the heroic practice of daily duty, with its thousand tiny details and small incidences. To be obstinately faithful to one's daily duty, without ever allowing the slightest voluntary infraction, supposes a constant heroism, which can only be provided to the soul by the intense action of the gift of fortitude.

[149] See *Novissima verba*, May 29.

Beatitudes and the Fruits Derived from It

St. Thomas, following St. Augustine, attributes to the gift of fortitude the fourth Beatitude—"Blessed are those who hunger and thirst for holiness, for they shall have their fill" (Matt. 5:6)— because fortitude is about arduous and difficult things; to desire to sanctify oneself, not in any way, but with true hunger and thirst, is extremely arduous and difficult, and so we see, in fact, that souls dominated by the gift of fortitude have an insatiable desire to do and suffer great things for God.[150] Already in this world they begin to receive their reward in the growth of the virtues and the most intense spiritual joys with which God often fills their souls.

The fruits of the Holy Spirit that respond to this gift are patience and long-suffering. The first, to endure with heroism the sufferings and evils; the second, not to lose heart in the prolonged practice of the good.[151]

Opposing Vices

According to St. Gregory, the gift of fortitude is opposed to disordered fear or timidity, often accompanied by a certain natural laziness, which comes from the love of one's own comfort, prevents us from undertaking great things for the glory of God and drives us to flee from abjection and pain.[152]

Lallemant writes:

> One cannot say how many omissions fear makes us guilty of. There are very few people who do for God and for their neighbor all that they could do. It is necessary to imitate the saints, fearing only sin, like St. John Chrysostom; facing all kinds of risks and

---

[150] See STh II–II, q. 139 a. 2.
[151] Ibid., ad 3.
[152] See *Morales*, c. 49: PL 75, 593.

dangers, like St. Francis Xavier; desiring affronts and
persecutions, like St. Ignatius.[153]

Means of Fostering This Gift

In addition to the general means for fostering the gifts (recollection,
prayer, fidelity to grace, invoking the Holy Spirit, and so on), the
following, among many others, closely affect the gift of fortitude:

1. Become accustomed to the exact fulfillment of
    duty in spite of all the repugnance. There are her-
    oisms that perhaps are not within our reach with
    the forces at our disposal at present; but there is
    no doubt that, with the simple help of the ordi-
    nary grace that God does not deny to anyone, we
    could do much more than what we do. We can
    never, by far, reach the heroism of the saints until
    the gift of fortitude acts intensely in us; but this
    action is not usually produced by the Holy Spirit
    to reward voluntary laziness and sloth. He who
    does what he can will not lack the help of God;
    but no one can complain of not experiencing it if
    he does not even do what he can.

2. Do not ask God to take the cross from us, but only
    to give us the strength to bear it in holiness. The
    gift of fortitude is given to the saints so that they
    can resist the great crosses and tribulations through
    which anyone who wants to reach the summit of
    sanctity must inevitably pass. Now, if upon experi-
    encing any pain or feeling the weight of a cross that
    Providence sends us, we begin to complain and ask

---

[153] L. Lallemant, *The Spiritual Doctrine*, princ. 4 c. 4 a. 6.

The Great Unknown

God to take it away from us, what cause will we
have to marvel when the gifts of the Holy Spirit do
not come to our help? If, in testing us in small
things, God finds us weak, how can He go forward
in His divine purifying action? Let us not complain
about our crosses; let us only ask the Lord to give
us the strength to bear them, and let us wait calmly,
for God's hour will soon come. He will never let
Himself be defeated in generosity.

3. Practice, with courage or weakness, voluntary
    mortifications. There is nothing that strengthens
    against the cold as much as getting used to living
    in the open. He who voluntarily embraces pain
    ends up not trembling before it and even finds
    true pleasure in experiencing it. It is not a matter
    of destroying ourselves with the blows of disci-
    pline or of practicing the great macerations of
    many saints: the soul is not yet ready for that. But
    when it comes to those thousand little details of
    daily life—keeping silent when we feel the itch to
    speak, never complaining about the inclement
    weather, the quality of the food, and so on, being
    affectionate and helpful with unpleasant people,
    receiving with humility and patience the mockery,
    reprimands, and contradictions of others—we
    can and should undertake them with the help of
    ordinary grace. Nor is it necessary to feel coura-
    geous or strenuous in order to practice these
    things. They can be done even in the midst of our
    weakness and frailty. St. Thérèse of the Child Jesus
    was happy to feel so, because in this way she put

162

all her trust in God and expected everything from Him.

4. Seek in the Eucharist strength for our souls. The Eucharist is the bread of angels, but also the bread of the strong. How this divine food strengthens and comforts the soul! St. John Chrysostom says that we must rise from the sacred table with the strength of a lion to launch ourselves into all kinds of heroic works for the glory of God.[154] It is there that we come into direct and intimate contact with Christ, the true lion of Judah, who is pleased to transfuse into our souls something of His divine strength.

[154] *In Io. Hom.* 61, 3: PL 59, 260.

CHAPTER 10

The Gift of Piety

THE THIRD OF the gifts of the Holy Spirit, in ascending scale from lesser to greater, is the gift of piety. Its fundamental mission is to perfect the infused virtue of the same name—derived from the cardinal virtue of justice—by imbuing our relations with God and with our neighbor with the filial and fraternal sense that should regulate the treatment of the children of the same family toward their father and toward their brothers and sisters. The gift of piety communicates to us the spirit of the family of God. Let us study it carefully.[155]

Nature

The gift of piety is a supernatural habit infused by God with sanctifying grace to excite in our will, by instinct of the Holy Spirit, a filial affection toward God, considered as Father, and a feeling of universal brotherhood toward all men as our brothers and sons of the same Father, who is in Heaven.

The following should be noted in connection with this definition:

1. The gift of piety, as the affective gift that it is, resides in the will as a power of the soul.

---

[155] See our *Theology of Christian Perfection*, n. 407–412.

2. The gift of piety differs from the infused virtue of the same name in that the latter tends to God as Father, the same as the gift, but with a human modality—that is, regulated by reason enlightened by faith—whereas the gift does so by the instinct of the Holy Spirit—that is, with a divine modality, incomparably more perfect.

3. The gift of piety extends to all men as children of the same Father, who is in Heaven, and also to all that pertains to the worship of God, perfecting the virtue of religion to the utmost, and even to the whole matter of justice and the virtues annexed to it, fulfilling all its demands and obligations for a nobler motive and a higher formality—namely, considering them as duties to their brothers and sisters, who are sons and relatives of God. Just as the virtue of piety is the family virtue par excellence, on a higher and more universal plane, it is the gift of the same name that is responsible for uniting and congregating, under the loving gaze of the Heavenly Father, the whole great family of the children of God.

Importance and Necessity

The gift of piety is absolutely necessary to perfect to the point of heroism the matter pertaining to the virtue of justice and all its derivatives, especially religion and piety, on which it falls in a more immediate and principal way.

How different it is, for example, to worship God solely under the impulse of the virtue of religion, which presents Him to us as Creator and sovereign Owner of all that exists, than to worship Him out of the instinct of the gift of piety, which makes us see in Him a most loving Father who loves us with infinite tenderness! The things of the service of God—worship, prayer, sacrifice, and so on—are fulfilled almost effortlessly, with exquisite perfection and delicacy: it is the service of the Father, no longer of the God of tremendous majesty.

In the treatment of men, what a note of refinement and exquisiteness the endearing feeling that we are all brothers and sons of the same Father adds to the already sublime demands of charity and justice!

Even with regard to the same material things, how everything changes! For those who are profoundly governed by the gift of mercy, the earth and the whole of creation is the house of the Father, in which everything that exists speaks to them of Him and of His infinite tenderness.

They effortlessly discover the religious meaning that beats in all things. All of them, even the wolf, the trees, the flowers, and death itself, are our brothers and sisters (as St. Francis affirms). It is then that the Christian virtues acquire a very delicate nuance, of exquisite perfection and completion, which it would be useless to demand of them without the influence of the gift of piety. Without the gifts of the Holy Spirit, let us repeat once again, no infused virtue can reach its perfect development and expansion.

Lallemant says in this regard:

> Piety has a great extension in the exercise of Christian justice. It is projected not only on God, but on all that is related to Him, such as the Sacred Scriptures, which contain His word; the blessed, who possess Him in glory; the souls in Purgatory, who purify themselves for Him; the men of the earth, who walk toward Him. He gives the spirit of a son to those who are superior,

the spirit of a father to those who are inferior, the spirit of a brother to those who are equal, the bowels of compassion for those who suffer and a tender inclination to rescue and help them.... It is He who makes us suffer with the afflicted, weep with those who weep, rejoice with those who rejoice, bear with gentleness the weaknesses of the sick and the faults of the imperfect; in short, to become all things to all, like the great apostle St. Paul (1 Cor. 9:22).[156]

Effects

The effects produced in the soul by the intense action of the gift of piety are marvelous. Here are the main ones:

Firstly, a great filial tenderness toward the Father who is in Heaven. This is the primary and fundamental effect. The soul understands perfectly and lives with ineffable sweetness those words of St. Paul: "For you did not receive the spirit of slavery to fall back into fear, but you have received the spirit of sonship. When we cry, 'Abba! Father!' it is the Spirit himself bearing witness with our spirit that we are children of God" (Rom. 8:15–16).

St. Thérèse of the Child Jesus, in whom, as is well known, the gift of piety shone to a sublime degree, could not think of this without weeping with love:

> When a novice entered her cell one day, she was surprised by the celestial expression on her face. She was sewing with great activity, and yet she seemed absorbed in deep contemplation. "What are you thinking about?" asked the young sister. "I am meditating on the Our Father," she answered. "It is so

[156] L. Lallemant, *La doctrine spirituelle*, princ. 4 c.4.

sweet to call God our Father!" As she said this, tears
glistened in her eyes.[157]

Dom Columba Marmion, the famous abbot of Meredsous, also possessed to a high degree this feeling of our adoptive divine filiation.
For him, God is, more than anything, our Father. The monastery
is the house of the Father, and all its inhabitants form the family
of God. The same must be said of the whole world and of all men.
He repeatedly insists, in all his works, on the need to cultivate this
spirit of adoption, which must be the fundamental attitude of the
Christian before God. He himself mentally asked for this spirit of
adoption when he bowed in the Gloria at the end of each psalm.[158]
Here is a splendid text from his precious work, *Jesus Christ in His
mysteries*, which admirably summarizes his thought:

> Let us never forget that the whole Christian life, like all
> holiness, is reduced to being by grace what Jesus is by
> nature: Son of God. Hence the sublimity of our reli-
> gion. The source of all the pre-eminence of Jesus, the
> value of all His states, of the fruitfulness of all His
> mysteries, is in His divine generation and in His quality
> of being the Son of God. Therefore, the most exalted
> saint in Heaven will be the one who in this world is the
> best son of God, the one who best brings to fruition the
> grace of supernatural adoption in Jesus Christ.[159]

The favorite prayer of these souls is the Our Father. They find in
it unfathomable treasures of doctrine and ineffable sweetness of

[157] See *History of a Soul*, 12, 4.
[158] We owe these data to the precious study of R. Thibaut, *Un maître
spirituelle: Dom Columba Marmion* (Paris: Desclée, 1929), c. 16.
[159] Columba Marmion, *Jesus Christ in His Mysteries*, 3, 1.

devotion, as it happened to St. Teresa of Jesus: "Let me hope to see that in so few words all contemplation and perfection is enclosed, that it seems we do not need any other book, but to study in this one,"[160] and her angelic daughter St. Thérèse of the Child Jesus writes that the Our Father and the Hail Mary "are the only prayers that elevate me, that nourish my soul to the divine; they are enough for me."[161]

Secondly, it makes us adore the ineffable mystery of the divine intra-trinitarian paternity. In its highest and most sublime manifestations, the gift of piety makes us penetrate into the mystery of the intimate life of God, giving us a very lively feeling, full of respect and adoration, of the divine paternity of the Father with respect to the eternal Word. It is no longer only a question of His spiritual fatherhood over us through grace, but of His divine fatherhood, eternally fruitful in the bosom of the Most Blessed Trinity. The soul delights with ineffable sweetness in the mystery of the eternal generation of the Word, which constitutes, if it is licit to speak in this way, the very happiness of God, and before this sovereign perspective, always eternal and always actual, the soul feels the need to annihilate itself, to be silent and to love, with no other language than that of adoration and tears. It likes to repeat in the depths of its spirit that sublime expression of the Gloria of the Mass: "We thank you for your immense glory" (*propter magnam gloriam tuam*). It is the worship and adoration of the divine Majesty in itself, without any relation to the benefits that we may have received from it. It is pure love, in all its awesome grandeur, without any admixture of selfish human elements.

[160] *Way of Perfection*, 37, 1.
[161] *Story of a Soul*, 10, 19.

Thirdly, a filial abandonment in the arms of the Heavenly Father. Intimately penetrated with the feeling of its adoptive divine filiation, the soul abandons itself calmly and confidently in the arms of its Heavenly Father. Nothing worries it nor is capable of disturbing for an instant the unalterable peace it enjoys. It asks nothing and rejects nothing in regard to its health or sickness, short or long life, consolations or aridity, energy or weakness, persecutions or praises, and so forth; it abandons itself totally in the arms of God, and the only thing it asks and desires is to glorify Him with all its strength, that all men might recognize its adoptive divine filiation and behave as true children of God, praising and glorifying the Father who is in Heaven.

Fourthly, it makes us see in our neighbor a child of God and a brother in Jesus Christ. It is a natural consequence of the adoptive filiation of grace. If God is our Father, we are all sons of God and brothers in Christ, in act or at least in potential. But how strongly they perceive and live this truth!

So sublime are the souls dominated by the gift of piety! They love all men with passionate tenderness, seeing in them the dearest brothers in Christ, whom they would like to shower with all kinds of graces and blessings. St. Paul's soul overflowed with this sentiment when he wrote to the Philippians: "Therefore, my brethren, whom I love and long for, my joy and crown, stand firm thus in the Lord, my beloved" (Phil. 4:1). Motivated by these tender sentiments, the soul devotes itself to all kinds of works of mercy toward the unfortunate, considering them as true brothers and sisters and serving them to please the Father of all. All the sacrifices demanded by the service of his neighbor, even the ungrateful, seem little to him. In each one of them he sees Christ, the elder brother, and he does for him what he would do for Christ Himself, and all that he does, though often heroic and superhuman, seems to him so natural and simple that he would be greatly astonished and would find it very strange if someone were to consider it as if it had some superb value: "But he is my brother," he would simply reply. All his movements and operations in the service of his neighbor are carried out with the common Father in mind, as proper and due to brothers and relatives of God (Eph. 2:19), and this makes all of them become acts of religion in a sublime and eminent way. Even the love and piety he professes for his relatives and blood relations are deeply penetrated by this higher and more sublime vision, which presents them as children of God and brothers and sisters in Jesus Christ.

Finally, we are moved to love and devotion for persons and things related in some way to the fatherhood of God or the Christian fraternity. By virtue of the gift of piety, filial love is perfected in the soul toward the Blessed Virgin Mary, whom it considers as the most tender Mother and with whom it has all the confidence and daring of a son toward the best of mothers.

He loves with tenderness the angels and saints, who are his older brothers and sisters, who already enjoy the continuous presence of the Father in the eternal mansion of the children of God. He attends to and assists the souls in Purgatory with continuous aid, considering them as dear brothers and sisters who suffer. To the pope, the gentle "Christ on earth," who is the visible head of the Church and father of all Christendom; to the superiors, in whom he sees, above all, their character as fathers more than in that of chiefs or inspectors, serving and obeying them in everything with true filial joy; to his homeland, which he would like to see imbued with the spirit of Jesus Christ in its laws and customs and for which he would gladly shed his blood, like St. Joan of Arc; to Sacred Scripture, which he reads with the same respect and love as if it were a letter from the Father sent from Heaven to tell him what he must do or what He wants of him; to holy things, especially those that belong to the worship and service of God (sacred vessels, monstrances, etc.), in which he sees the instruments of the Father's service and glorification — to all of these, he feels an immense and abiding love.

Beatitudes and the Fruits Derived from It

According to St. Thomas, three of the Gospel Beatitudes are intimately related to the gift of piety:

1. Blessed are the meek, for meekness removes impediments to the exercise of piety.

2. Blessed are those who hunger and thirst for righteousness, for the gift of piety perfects the works of the virtue of righteousness and all its derivatives.

3. Blessed are the merciful, for mercy is also exercised in corporal and spiritual works of mercy.[162]

Of the fruits of the Holy Spirit, kindness and gentleness are to be attributed directly to the gift of piety, and meekness indirectly, insofar as it removes impediments to acts of piety.[163]

Opposing Vices

The vices that oppose the gift of piety can be grouped under the generic name of impiety. For since it is precisely to the gift of piety that it belongs to offer to God with filial affection what belongs to Him as our Father, anyone who in one way or another willfully violates this duty properly deserves the name of impious.

[162] See STh II–II, q. 121 a. 2.
[163] Ibid., ad 3.

On the other hand, "piety, as a gift, consists in a certain superhuman benevolence toward everyone,"[164] considering them as children of God and our brothers and sisters in Christ. For this reason, St. Gregory the Great opposes the gift of piety to hardness of the heart, which is born of disordered love for oneself.[165]

Fr. Lallemant has written an admirable page on this hardness of heart:

> The vice opposed to the gift of piety is hardness of heart, which is born of disordered love of ourselves: for this love causes us naturally to be sensitive to nothing but our own interests, and that nothing affects us but what relates to ourselves; that we see the offenses of God without tears, and the miseries of our neighbor without compassion; that we do not want to trouble ourselves in anything to help others; that we cannot bear their faults; that we lash out at them for any trifle, and that we retain toward them in our hearts feelings of bitterness and revenge, of hatred and antipathy. On the contrary, the more charity and love of God a soul has, the more sensitive it is to the interests of God and neighbor.
>
> This hardness is extreme in the great of the world, in the avaricious rich, in sensual persons, and in those who do not soften their hearts by exercises of piety and by the use of spiritual things. It is also frequently found in the wise who do not combine devotion with knowledge, and who, in order to flatter themselves with this defect, call it solidity of spirit; but the truly

[164] St. Thomas Aquinas, III *Sent.* d. 9 q. 1 a. 1.
[165] See *Morales*, c. 49: PL 75, 593; see STh I–II, q. 68 a. 2 ad 3; a. 6 ad 2; II–II q. 159 a. 2 ad 1.

wise have been the most pious, such as St. Augustine,
St. Thomas, St. Bonaventure, St. Bernard, and in the
Society, Laínez, Suárez, Belarmine, Lesio.

A soul that cannot weep for its sins, at least with
the tears of the heart, has a great deal of impiety or
impurity, or both at the same time, as happens ordinarily to those whose hearts are hardened.

It is a great misfortune when natural and acquired
talents are more esteemed in religion than piety. You
will often see religious, and perhaps superiors, who will
say aloud that they pay much more heed to a spirit capable of attending to many affairs than to all those little
devotions, which are, they say, good for women, but
unbecoming of a sound spirit, calling this hardness of
heart, so opposed to the gift of piety, "soundness of
spirit." They ought to think that devotion is an act of
the virtue of religion, or a fruit of religion and charity,
and that, consequently, it is preferable to all the moral
virtues, since religion immediately follows, in order of
dignity, the theological virtues.

When a serious or respectable father by age or by
the offices he has held in religion testifies before
young religious that he esteems great talents and brilliant jobs, or that he prefers those who excel in schol-
arship or wit more than those who do not have so
much of these things, even if they have more virtue
and piety, he does great harm to these poor youth. It
is a poison that is injected into their hearts, and from
which perhaps they will never be cured. A word said
confidentially to another is capable of upsetting him
completely.[166]

---

[166] L. Lallemant, *The Spiritual Doctrine*, princ. 4 a. 3.

Means of Fostering This Gift

Apart from the general means of fostering the gifts of the Holy Spirit (recollection, prayer, fidelity to grace, etc.), the following are closely related to the gift of piety:

1. Cultivating in ourselves the spirit of being God's adopted children. There is no truth that is instilled in us so many times in the gospel as the truth that God is our Father. In the Sermon on the Mount alone, the Lord repeats it fourteen times. This attitude of children before the Father stands out so much in the New Law that some have wanted to see in it the most typical and essential note of Christianity.

    We cannot insist enough on fostering in our souls this spirit of filial trust and abandonment in the arms of our most loving Father. God is our Creator, He will be our judge at the hour of death; but, first and foremost, He is always our Father. The gift of fear inspires in us a respectful reverence, never fear in the negative sense, that is perfectly compatible with the filial tenderness and trust that the gift of mercy inspires in us. Only under the transforming action of this gift does the soul feel itself to be fully God's daughter and live with infinite sweetness its condition as such. But we can already do much to attain this spirit, disposing ourselves, with the help of grace, to remain always before God as a son before his most loving father. Let us continually ask for the spirit of adoption, linking this petition to whatever exercise we have to repeat many times a day, as we saw Dom Marmion do at every Gloria at the end of the psalms, and let us strive to do all things for the love of God, just to please our most loving Father, who is in Heaven.

2. Cultivating the spirit of universal fraternity with all men. This, as we have seen, is the principal secondary effect of the gift of piety. Before practicing it in all its fullness by the performance of the gift, we can do much on our part with the help of ordinary grace. Let us widen more each time the capacity of our heart until we are able to put in it the entire world of our interior love. We are all children of God and brothers and sisters of Jesus Christ. With what persuasive insistence St. Paul repeated this to the early Christians: "In Christ Jesus you are all sons of God, through faith. For as many of you as were baptized into Christ have put on Christ. There is neither Jew nor Greek, there is neither slave nor free, there is neither male nor female; for you are all one in Christ Jesus" (Gal. 3:26–28). If we did all we could to treat all our fellow men and women as true brothers and sisters in God, we would undoubtedly attract His merciful gaze, which delights in nothing so much as to see us all intimately united in His divine Son. Christ Himself wants the world to know that we are His disciples by our intimate love for one another (John 13:35).

3. Considering all things, even the purely material, as belonging to the Father's house, which is the whole of creation. What a profoundly religious

sense souls governed by the gift of piety find in all things! St. Francis of Assisi passionately embraced a tree because it was a brother of his in God. St. Paul of the Cross was ecstatic before the little flowers in his garden, which spoke to him of the Heavenly Father. St. Thérèse wept with tenderness when she contemplated a hen sheltering her chicks under her wings, remembering the Gospel image with which Christ wanted to show us the sentiments of His divine heart, even toward ungrateful and rebellious children (Matt. 23:37). Without going as far as these delicacies, which are proper to the gift of piety acting intensely, what a different meaning we could give to our dealings with creatures—even purely material ones—if we would strive to discover, in the light of faith, their religious aspect, which beats so deeply in all of them! The whole of creation is the Father's house, and all things in it belong to Him. With what delicacy we would treat even the purely material! We would discover in it something divine, which would make us respect it as if each creature were a sacred vessel. At what a distance from sin (which is always a sort of sacrilege against God or the things of God) would such an attitude place us before God! Our whole life would be elevated to a higher plane, reaching a sublime height before the most loving gaze of our Father in Heaven.

4. Cultivating the spirit of total abandonment in the arms of God. We will not achieve this in all its fullness until the gift of piety acts intensely in

us. But in the meantime, let us strive to do our part as much as we can. We must be fully convinced that, since God is our Father, it is impossible for anything bad to happen to us in all that He wills or permits to come upon us, and so we must remain indifferent to health or sickness, to long or short life, to peace or war, to consolations or aridity of spirit, and so forth, continually repeating our acts of surrender and abandonment to His most holy will. The fiat, the yes, the "whatever you will, Lord," should be the fundamental attitude of the Christian before God, in total and filial abandonment to His divine and paternal will, which can only desire for us the greatest good, even if at times this good has the appearance of evil before our purely human and natural gaze.

CHAPTER 11

The Gift of Counsel

ON JULY 25, 1956, a maritime disaster shocked the whole world. The best Italian ship, the *Andrea Doria*, sank in the Atlantic near the coast of New York. The cause? An oversight on the part of the helmsman, who did not know how to turn quickly enough when the Swedish ship *Stockolm* crossed his path.

If only we could know the accidents that happen every day and at all hours, through lack of direction or intuition, to the souls of men! The virtue of prudence, and especially the gift of counsel, which perfects it, will teach us how to overcome these serious inconveniences.[167]

Nature

The gift of counsel is a supernatural habit by which the soul in grace, under the inspiration of the Holy Spirit, rightly intuits, in particular cases, what should be done in order to achieve the ultimate supernatural end.

The following should be noted in particular in connection with this definition:

---

[167] See our *Theology of Christian Perfection*, n. 381–86.

1. The gifts of the Holy Spirit are not transient motions or simple present graces, but supernatural habits infused by God into the soul together with sanctifying grace.

2. The Holy Spirit sets in motion the gift of counsel as the sole motive cause, but the soul in grace collaborates as an instrumental cause, through the virtue of prudence, to produce a supernatural act, which will proceed, as regards the substance of the act, from the virtue of prudence, and, as regards its divine modality, from the gift of counsel. This same mechanism is at work in the other gifts. This is why His acts are carried out promptly and as if by instinct, without the need for the slow and laborious work of the discourse of reason (Matt. 10:19–20).

3. Supernatural prudence judges correctly what must be done at a given moment, guided by the lights of reason enlightened by faith. But the gift of counsel quickly intuits what must be done under the instinct and motion of the Holy Spirit — that is, for entirely divine reasons, which are often ignored by the very soul that performs that act. That is why the mode of action is discursive in the virtue of prudence, while in the gift it is intuitive, divine or superhuman.

Importance and Necessity

The intervention of the gift of counsel is indispensable for perfecting the virtue of prudence, especially in certain sudden, unforeseen, and difficult cases that require a rapid solution, since sin or heroism is a matter of an instant. These cases, which are less rare than is commonly believed, cannot be resolved with slow and laborious work of the virtue of prudence, going through its eight moments or fundamental aspects;[168] the intervention of the gift of counsel is necessary, which will give us the instantaneous solution of what must be done by that kind of instinct or connaturality characteristic of the gifts.

It is very difficult at times to reconcile gentleness with firmness, the need to keep a secret with the requirement to tell the truth, the interior life with the apostolate, affection with chastity, the prudence of the serpent with the simplicity of the dove (Matt. 10:16). For all these things, the lights of prudence are sometimes not enough; the intervention of the gift of counsel is required. Fr. Lallemant writes:

> There are in Sacred Scripture a multitude of passages in which the intervention of the gift of counsel is clearly seen, as in the silence of our Lord before Herod; in the admirable answer He gave to save the adulterous woman and to confound those who maliciously asked Him if tribute was to be paid to Caesar; in the trial of Solomon; in the undertaking of Judith to deliver the people of God from the army of Holofernes; in the conduct of Daniel to justify Susanna from the calumny of the two old men; in that of St. Paul when he set Pharisees and Sadducees against each other and when he appealed to Caesar's tribunal, and so on.[169]

---

[168] They are the following: memory of the past, intelligence of the present, docility, sagacity, reasoning, Providence, circumspection, and caution (see STh II–II, q. 49 a. 1–8).

[169] L. Lallemant, *The Spiritual Doctrine*, princ. 4, c. 4, a. 4.

Effects

The effects that the gift of counsel produces in those fortunate souls in whom it acts are admirable. Here are some of the most important ones:

First, it preserves us from the danger of a false conscience. It is very easy to delude oneself on this delicate point, especially if one has a profound knowledge of moral theology. There is hardly any disordered passion that cannot be justified in some way by invoking some principle of morality, perhaps very true and sure in itself, but badly applied to that particular case. It is more difficult for the ignorant person, but those that are technical and knowledgeable can easily find a "title" to justify the unjustifiable. St. Augustine rightly said that "what we want is good, and what we like is holy." Only the intervention of the gift of counsel—which, overcoming the lights of natural reason, darkened by caprice or passion, dictates what is to be done with unappealable certainty and force—can preserve us from this very serious error of confusing light with darkness. In this sense, no one needs the gift of counsel more than wise men and theologians, who can so easily delude themselves, falsely placing their science at the service of their own comforts and whims.

Secondly, it solves for us, with ineffable certainty and success, a multitude of difficult and unforeseen situations. We have already said that sometimes the lights of simple supernatural prudence are not enough. It is necessary to resolve on the spot very difficult situations which, theoretically, could not be solved in several hours of study, and on whose right or wrong solution perhaps depends the salvation of a soul (e.g., a priest administering the last sacraments to a dying person). In these difficult cases, souls who are habitually faithful to grace and submissive to the action of the Holy Spirit suddenly receive the inspiration of the gift of counsel, which resolves that very difficult situation on the spot with a truly admirable certainty and firmness. This surprising phenomenon occurred many times in the life of the holy Curé d'Ars, who, in spite of his scant theological knowledge, resolved and instantly confessed, with admirable certainty and accuracy, difficult moral cases that would astound the most eminent theologians.

Thirdly, it inspires us with the most opportune means to govern others in a holy manner. The influence of the gift of counsel always refers to concrete and particular cases. But it is not limited to the purely private and personal regime of our own actions; it also extends to the correct direction of others, especially in unforeseen and difficult cases. How much prudence is needed for the superior to reconcile the filial affection, which he must always try to inspire in his subjects, with the energy and fortitude to demand compliance with the law, to combine kindness with justice, to get his subjects to fulfill their duty out of love, without piling up precepts, commands, and reprimands! The spiritual director, how will he be able to resolve with certainty and wisdom the thousand little conflicts that trouble poor souls, to advise them what they should do in each case, to decide in matters of vocation when it appears doubtful, and to guide each soul on its own path to God? It is scarcely conceivable that such wisdom could be achieved without the frequent and energetic intervention of the gift of counsel.

There were saints who had this gift to the highest degree. St. Anthony of Florence was so remarkable for the admirable inspiration of his advice that he has gone down in history with the nickname of Antoninus Consiliorum, Anthony the Counselor. St. Catherine of Siena was the pope's right arm and best adviser. Joan of Arc, without possessing military training, drew plans and directed operations that astonished the most expert captains, who saw their military prudence infinitely surpassed by that poor woman. St. Thérèse of the Child Jesus carried out with exquisite skill, in her youth, the difficult and delicate position of novice mistress, which requires so much maturity and experience.

Fourthly, it extraordinarily increases our docility and submission to our legitimate superiors. Here is an admirable effect, which at first sight seems incompatible with the gift of counsel, but which, nevertheless, is one of its most natural and spontaneous consequences. It would seem that the soul governed directly by the Holy Spirit would have no obligation or need to consult with men about its affairs. And yet the opposite is true: no one is so docile and submissive, no one has such a strong inclination to ask for the advice of God's legitimate representatives on earth (superiors, spiritual director, and so on) as souls subjected to the action of the gift of counsel.

It is because the Holy Spirit urges them to do so. God has determined that man should be ruled and governed by men. In Sacred Scripture we have innumerable examples of this. St. Paul falls from his horse, knocked down by the divine light, but he is not told what to do, but only to go into the city, and Ananias will tell him from God (see Acts 9:1–6). God uses this same style of communication with all His saints: He inspires them with humility, submission, and obedience to His legitimate representatives on earth. In case of conflict between what He inspires in them and what the superior or director commands, He wants them to obey the latter. He expressly told St. Teresa: "Whenever the Lord commanded me something in prayer, if the confessor told me something else, the Lord Himself would tell me to obey him; then His Majesty would return to him so that he would command me again."[170] Even when, with such a lack of judgment, some confessors ordered St. Teresa to mock the apparitions of the Lord (considering them diabolical), the Lord Himself told her to obey without reply: "Tell me that nothing should

[170] *Life*, 26, 5.

be given to me, that I did well to obey, but that He would make the truth be understood."[171] The saint learned the lesson so well that when the Lord ordered her to do something, she immediately consulted her confessors, without telling them that the Lord had commanded it (so as not to coerce their freedom of judgment); and only after they had decided what was to be done did she give them an account of the divine communication, if both things coincided; and if not, she asked the Lord to change the confessor's mind, while in the meantime obeying her superior.

This is one of the clearest and most manifest signs of good spirit, showing clearly that the communications that are believed to be received from God are really from Him. Revelation or vision that inspires rebellion and disobedience needs no further examination to be rejected as false or diabolical.

Beatitudes and the Fruits Derived from It

Augustine assigns to the gift of counsel the fifth Beatitude, corresponding to the merciful (see Matt. 5:7). But St. Thomas admits it only in a directive sense, insofar as the gift of counsel falls on things useful or convenient for salvation, and nothing so useful as mercy for others. But in an executive sense, mercy corresponds, as we have seen, to the gift of piety.

Insofar as it is related to mercy, the gift of counsel corresponds in some way to the fruits of goodness and kindness.[172]

Opposing Vices

The gift of counsel is opposed, by defect, to haste in acting, following the impulse of natural activity, without giving place to consult

---

[171] Ibid., 29, 6.
[172] See STh II–II, q. 52 a. 4; q. 121 a. 2; q. 52 a. 4 ad 3.

the Holy Spirit; and to rashness, which implies a lack of attention to the lights of faith and to divine inspiration because of excessive confidence in oneself and in one's own strength. Slowness is also opposed to the gift of counsel because, although it is necessary to use mature reflection before acting, once a determination has been made according to the lights of the Holy Spirit, it is necessary to proceed quickly to execution before circumstances change and occasions are lost.[173]

Means of Fostering This Gift

Apart from those already mentioned for the general promotion of the gifts (recollection, life of prayer, fidelity to grace), which cannot be overemphasized, the following means will greatly help us to prepare ourselves for the performance of the gift of counsel when it is needed.

1. Deep humility to recognize our ignorance and our need for enlightenment by the Spirit. The humble and persevering prayer has irresistible force before the mercy of God. It is necessary to invoke the Holy Spirit in the morning when we get up to ask for His guidance and counsel throughout the day; at the beginning of every action, with a simple and brief movement of the heart, which will be, at the same time, an act of love; in difficult or dangerous moments, in which, more than ever, we need the light from Heaven; before making an important determination or issuing some guiding judgment for others, and so on.

[173] L. Lallemant, *The Spiritual Doctrine*, princ. 4, c. 4, a. 4.

2. To accustom ourselves to always proceed with reflection and without haste. All human industry
   and diligence will prove insufficient to act pru-
   dently, as we have already said; but God does not
   withhold His grace from those who do what they
   can. When it is necessary, the gift of counsel will
   act without fail to make up for our ignorance and
   impotence; but let us not tempt God by expecting
   by divine means what we can do ourselves with
   the help of ordinary grace.

3. To attend in silence to the interior Master. If we
   succeeded in creating a vacuum in our spirit and
   completely silenced the noises of the world, we
   would often hear the voice of God, who in solitude often speaks to the heart (Hos 2:14). The
   soul must flee from the external turmoil and
   completely quiet its spirit in order to hear the
   lessons of eternal life that the Divine Master will
   explain to it, as He once did to Mary of Bethany,
   quiet and tranquil at His feet (see Luke 10:39).
   Philipon writes in this regard:

   > The Christian should walk through this
   > world with his eyes fixed on the sublime des-
   > tiny that awaits him: the consummation of
   > his life in the unity of the Trinity, in society
   > with the Father, the Son, and the Holy
   > Spirit, with other men, his brothers, and
   > with the angels, who are also called to dwell
   > with us in the same City of God, forming all
   > together a single divine family: the Church
   > of the incarnate Word, the total Christ.

Why does not all our moral activity spring in us from this supreme orientation of our existence toward the Beatific Vision of the Trinity? We crawl in an atmosphere of vanities, of merely earthly horizons, and yet, the grace of God allows us to divinize our acts and to enhance them down to their smallest details, raising them to the level of the intentions of Christ, a level on which we should maintain ourselves without faltering, conscious of our divine filiation.

Our lives should develop, in all their moments, at the breath of the Spirit of the Father and of the Son, without ever deviating toward evil, without ever delaying their impulse toward God. The Holy Spirit is not only very close to us, but also within us, in the depths of our souls, to enlighten us with the clarities of God, to inspire us to carry out actions that are entirely divine, to facilitate their fulfillment. The more a soul surrenders itself to the Holy Spirit, the more it is divinized. Perfect holiness consists in refusing nothing to love.[174]

4. Extreme docility and obedience to those whom God has placed in the Church to govern us. Let us imitate the examples of the saints. St. Teresa, as we have seen, obeyed her confessors in preference to the Lord Himself, and the Lord praised her conduct. The docile, obedient, humble soul

[174] M. M. Philipon, *The Gifts of the Holy Spirit*, 281.

is in the best condition to receive enlightenment from on high. There is nothing, on the contrary, that so distances us from the mysterious echo of the voice of God as a spirit of self-sufficiency and insubordination to His legitimate representatives on earth.

CHAPTER 12

The Gift of Knowledge

THE FIFTH GIFT of the Holy Spirit, following the ascending scale from lesser to greater perfection, is the gift of knowledge, which we will carefully study below.[175]

Some authors assign to the gift of knowledge the mission of perfecting the virtue of hope. But St. Thomas attributes it to faith, assigning to hope the gift of fear, as we have already seen. We follow this criterion of the Angelic Doctor, which is based, it seems to us, on the very nature of the gift of knowledge.[176]

Nature

The gift of knowledge is a supernatural habit infused by God with sanctifying grace, by which man's intelligence, under the illuminating action of the Holy Spirit, judges rightly of created things ordered toward the supernatural ultimate end.

Let us explain the terms of this synthetic definition to better understand the true nature of this admirable gift.

> 1. It is a supernatural habit infused by God with
>   sanctifying grace. It is not a question of human or

[175] See our *Theology of Christian Perfection*, n. 343–48.
[176] See STh II–II, q. 9 and q. 19.

philosophical science, which gives rise to a certain
and evident knowledge of things deduced by natural reasoning from their principles or their proximate or remote causes. Nor is it a question of
theological science, which deduces from the truths
revealed by God the virtualities they contain by
means of natural discourse or reasoning. Rather, it
is a certain supernatural knowledge proceeding
from a special enlightenment of the Holy Spirit,
which unveils and makes us rightly appreciate the
connection of created things with the supernatural
ultimate end. More briefly: it is the right estimation of the present temporal life ordered toward
eternal life. It is an infused, supernatural habit, inseparable from grace, which is essentially distinguished from acquired habits, from natural
science, and from theology.

2. By which man's intelligence. The gift of knowledge, as a habit, resides in the understanding, as
   does the virtue of faith, which it perfects, and it is
   primarily speculative, and secondarily practical.

3. Under the illuminating action of the Holy Spirit.
   It is the agent cause that sets in motion the supernatural habit of the gift. By virtue of this divine motion, very different from ordinary actual
   grace that sets the virtues in motion, human intelligence apprehends and judges created things
   by a certain divine instinct, by a certain connaturality, which the just person potentially possesses,
   by the theological virtues, with all that belongs
   to God. Under the action of this gift, man does
   not proceed by laborious reasoning, but judges

rightly of everything created by a higher impulse and a higher light than that of simple reason illuminated by faith.

4. Judges rightly. This is the formal reason that distinguishes the gift of knowledge from the gift of understanding. The latter, as we shall see, has the purpose of grasping and penetrating revealed truths by a profound supernatural intuition, but without passing judgment on them (simplex intuitus veritatis). That of knowledge, on the other hand, under the special impulse of the Holy Spirit, judges created things correctly in order to attain the ultimate supernatural end, and in this it also differs from the gift of wisdom, whose function is to judge divine things, not created things. Lallemant writes:

> Wisdom and knowledge have something in common. Both make God and creatures known. But when God is known through creatures and when we rise from the knowledge of second causes to the first and universal cause, it is an act of knowledge, and when one knows human things by the taste one has of God and judges of created beings by the knowledge one has of the first being, it is an act of wisdom.[177]

5. Of created things ordered toward the supernatural ultimate end. It is, as we have already said, the material object upon which the gift of

---

[177] L. Lallemant, *The Spiritual Doctrine*, princ. 4 c. 4 a. 3; see STh II–II, q. 9 a. 1 ad 3.

> knowledge falls, and since created things can be
> related to the end either by impelling us toward
> it or by trying to turn us away from it, the gift of
> knowledge gives the just man the right to judge
> in both senses.[178]

Moreover, the gift of knowledge extends also to the divine things that are contemplated in creatures, coming from God, for the manifestation of His glory, according to St. Paul: "His invisible nature, namely, his eternal power and deity, has been clearly perceived in the things that have been made" (Rom. 1:20).[179] John of St. Thomas writes:

> This right judgment of creatures is the knowledge of
> the saints; and it is founded on that spiritual taste and
> affection of charity which does not rest in God alone,
> but is also passed on to creatures by God, ordering
> them to Him and forming a judgment of them ac-
> cording to their properties, that is, by the lower and
> created causes; wisdom being distinguished in this,
> which starts from the supreme cause, being united to
> it by charity.[180]

Importance and Necessity

The gift of knowledge is absolutely necessary for faith to reach its full expression and development in a different aspect from that which corresponds, as we shall see, to the gift of understanding. It is not enough to apprehend revealed truth, even with that profound and intuitive penetration that the gift of understanding provides;

---

[178] See STh II, q. 9 a. 4.
[179] See ibid., a. 2 ad 3.
[180] See John of St. Thomas, *Cursus theologicus*, I–II d. 18 a. 43 n. 10.

we must also be given a supernatural instinct to discover and judge correctly the relationship of these divine truths with the natural and sensible world around us. Without this supernatural instinct, faith itself would be in danger, for, attracted and seduced by the charm of created things and ignorant of the way to relate them to the supernatural world, we would easily wander from the path, abandoning, at least practically, the light of faith and throwing ourselves, with a blindfold over our eyes, into the arms of the mundane created world. Daily experience confirms all this too much.

The gift of knowledge, therefore, renders inestimable services to the Faith, especially in practice. For by it, under the prompting and enlightenment of the Holy Spirit and by a certain affinity and connaturality with spiritual things, we judge rightly, according to the principles of faith, of the use of creatures, and of their value, usefulness, or dangers for eternal life, so that those who work under the influence of this gift can be said with great propriety and accuracy to have received from God the "knowledge of the saints": *dedit illi scientiam sanctorum* (Wis. 10:10).

Effects

The effects produced in the soul by the action of the gift of knowledge are admirable and varied, all of them of great sanctifying value. Here are the main ones:

Firstly, it teaches us to judge rightly of created things ordered toward God. This is proper and specific to the gift of knowledge. Philipon writes:

> Under its impulse, a double movement takes place in the soul: the experience of the emptiness of the creature, of its nothingness; and also, at the sight of creation, the discovery of God's imprint. The same gift of

knowledge brought tears to St. Dominic's eyes when he thought of the fate of poor sinners, while the spectacle of nature inspired St. Francis of Assisi's famous Canticle of the Sun. The two sentiments appear in the well-known passage of the Spiritual Canticle of St. John of the Cross, where the saint describes the relief and at the same time the torment of the mystical soul at the sight of creation, when the things of the universe reveal to it the passage of its Beloved, while He remains invisible until the soul, transformed into Him, meets Him in the Beatific Vision.[181]

The first aspect made St. Ignatius of Loyola exclaim when he contemplated the spectacle of a starry night: "Oh, how vile the earth seems to me when I contemplate the sky!" The second made St. John of the Cross fall in rapture before the beauty of a fountain, of a mountain, of a landscape, of a sunset, or when listening to "the whistling of the misty air." The nothingness of created things, contemplated through the gift of knowledge, led St. Paul to consider them all as garbage in order to win Christ (Phil. 3:8); and the beauty of God, reflected in the beauty and fragrance of flowers, compelled St. Paul of the Cross to say to them amidst transports of love: "Be silent, little flowers, be silent. . . ." This same sentiment is what gave the Poverello of Assisi that sublime sense of universal fraternity with all things from the hands of God: brother sun, brother wolf, sister flower, and so on. It was also the gift of knowledge that gave St. Teresa that amazing facility to explain the things of God using comparisons and similarities taken from created things.

[181] M. M. Philipon, *The Spiritual Doctrine of Sister Elizabeth of the Trinity*, c. 8, n. 6.

Secondly, knowledge guides us with certainty as to what we must believe or not believe. The souls in whom the gift of knowledge acts intensely have instinctively the sense of faith. Without having studied theology or being lettered in any way, these souls realize on the spot whether a devotion, a doctrine, a piece of advice, any maxim, is in agreement and in tune with the Faith or not. Do not ask them the reasons they have for it, for they do not know them. They feel it with an irresistible force and an unshakable certainty. It is admirable how St. Teresa, in spite of her humility and surrendered submission to her confessors, could never accept the erroneous doctrine that in certain elevated states of prayer it is convenient to dispense with the consideration of the adored humanity of Christ.[182]

Thirdly, it makes us see with promptness and certainty the state of our soul. Everything appears transparent and clear to the penetrating introspection of the gift of knowledge: "our interior acts, the secret movements of our heart, its qualities, its goodness, its malice, its principles, its motives, its ends and intentions, its effects and consequences, its merit and its demerit."[183] St. Teresa rightly said that "in a room where much sun enters there is no hidden spider's web."[184]

Fourthly, it inspires us in the most correct way to conduct ourselves with our neighbor in order to attain eternal life. In this sense, the gift of knowledge, in its practical aspect, makes its influence felt on the virtue of prudence itself, the direct perfection of which, as we have seen, is the gift of counsel. Fr. Lallemant writes:

[182] Here are his own words: "And although they have contradicted me in it and said that I do not understand it, because they are paths where our Lord leads, and that when they have already passed from the principles it is better to deal in things of the Divinity and flee from corporeal things, they will not make me confess that it is a good way" (Sixth Dwelling, 7, 5; see *Life*, 22, where he explains his thought at length).
[183] L. Lallemant, *The Spiritual Doctrine*, princ. 4 c. 4 a. 3.
[184] *Life*, 19, 2.

A preacher knows by this gift what he should say to his listeners and how he should urge them. A director knows the state of the souls he directs, their spiritual needs, the remedies for their faults, the obstacles that oppose their perfection, the shortest and surest way to lead them, when to console or mortify them, what God works in them, and what they must do on their part to cooperate with God and fulfill His designs. A superior knows how to govern his subjects.

Those who partake most of the gift of knowledge are the most enlightened in all their knowledge. They see marvels in the practice of virtue. They discover degrees of perfection which are unknown to others. They see at a glance whether actions are inspired by God and conform to His designs; as soon as they deviate a little from the ways of God, they perceive it in the act. They point out imperfections where others cannot recognize them, and are not liable to be deceived in their feelings or to be surprised by the illusions of which the world is full. If a scrupulous soul addresses them, they will know what it is necessary to say to him in order to cure his scruples. If they are to address an exhortation to religious men or women, thoughts will come to their minds in conformity with the spiritual needs of these religious persons and the spirit of their order. If difficulties of conscience are proposed to them, they will solve them excellently. Ask them for the reason of their answer, and they will not say a single word to you, since they know all this without reason, by a light superior to all reasons.

Thanks to this gift, St. Vincent Ferrer preached with the prodigious success that we read about in his life. He abandoned himself to the Holy Spirit, whether to prepare his sermons or to deliver them, and everyone was impressed. It was easy to see that the Holy Spirit spoke through his mouth. One day when he was to preach before a prince, he felt that he should bring to the preparation of his sermon more human study and diligence. He did so with extraordinary interest; but neither the prince nor the rest of the audience were as satisfied with this studied preaching as with that of the following day, which he delivered, as usual, according to the movement of the Spirit of God. The difference between these two sermons was pointed out to him. "It is," he replied, "that yesterday Friar Vincent preached, and today it was the Holy Spirit."[185]

Fifthly, it detaches us from the things of the earth. In reality, this is nothing more than a logical consequence of that right judgment of things that constitutes the typical note of the gift of knowledge. "All creatures are as if they were not before God."[186] That is why we must go beyond them and transcend them in order to rest in God alone. But only the gift of knowledge gives the saints that profound vision of the need for absolute detachment that we admire, for example, in St. John of the Cross. For a soul enlightened by the gift of knowledge, creation is an open book, wherein the soul effortlessly discovers the nothingness of creatures and the absolute totality of the Creator. "The soul passes through the creatures without seeing them, only to stop in Christ.... The whole of all created things, is it worth even a glance for him who has felt God, even if only once?"[187]

[185] L. Lallemant, *The Spiritual Doctrine*, l.c.
[186] See St. John of the Cross, *Ascent*, I, 4, 3.
[187] M. M. Philipon, *The Gifts of the Holy Spirit*, l.c.

It is curious the effect that produced in St. Teresa the jewels that her friend Luisa de la Cerda showed her in Toledo. Here is the Teresian text with all its inimitable gallantry:

> Once when I was with that lady, being already bad at heart (because, as I have said, I had a bad heart, although it is no longer so), she made me take out jewels of gold and stones, which she placed great value upon, especially one of diamonds that she valued especially highly. She thought they would cheer me up. I was laughing to myself and feeling sorry to see what men value, remembering what the Lord has in store for us, and I thought how impossible it would be for me, even if I wanted to try to do it myself, to care for such higher things if the Lord did not take away the memory of these mundanities. This is a great mastery for the soul, so great that I do not know if anyone will understand it except the one who possesses it, because it is our own natural detachment, without any labor on our part. God does it all; His Majesty shows us these truths in such a way that they are so impressed, that it is clear that we could not acquire them for ourselves in such a short space of time.[188]

Sixthly, it teaches us to make a holy use of creatures. This sentiment, complementary to the previous one, is another natural and spontaneous derivation of the right judgment of created things, proper to the gift of knowledge. For it is true that the being of creatures is nothing compared to that of God, but it is no less true that "all

---

[188] St. Teresa of Jesus, *Life*, 38, 4.

creatures are crumbs that fell from God's table,"[189] and they speak to us of Him and lead us to Him when we know how to make appropriate use of them.

This is exactly what the gift of knowledge does. The examples are innumerable in the lives of the saints. The contemplation of created things led their souls back to God, whose imprint they saw in creatures. Any insignificant detail, unnoticed by ordinary mortals, made a strong impression on their souls, leading them to God.

Finally, it fills us with contrition and repentance for our past errors. This is another natural consequence of the right judgment of creatures. In the resplendent light of the gift of knowledge, we effortlessly discover the nothingness of creatures — their fragility, their vanity, their short duration, their inability to make us happy, the harm that attachment to them can bring to the soul — and, remembering other times in our life when we may have been subjected to so much vanity and misery, we feel in our innermost depths a very lively repentance, which bursts outwardly in very intense acts of contrition and self-contempt. The pathetic accents of the Miserere spring spontaneously from our souls as a psychological need and demand, which relieve us and unburden us a little of the weight that overwhelms us. This is why the Beatitude of those who weep corresponds to the gift of knowledge, as we shall see shortly.

Such, broadly speaking, are the principal effects of the gift of knowledge. Thanks to it, the virtue of faith, far from finding obstacles in creatures to reach God, makes use of them as a lever and aid to do so more easily. Perfected by the gifts of knowledge and understanding, the virtue of faith attains a very lively intensity, which makes the soul see with divine clarity the eternal vision.

[189] St. John of the Cross, *Ascent*, I, 6, 3.

Beatitudes and the Fruits Derived from It

The third Gospel Beatitude corresponds to the gift of knowledge: "Blessed are those who mourn, for they shall be comforted" (Matt. 5:4). This is both on the merit side and on the reward side. On the part of the merit (tears), because the gift of knowledge, insofar as it involves a right estimation of creatures ordered toward eternal life, impels the just man to mourn his past errors and illusions in the use of creatures, and on the part of the reward (consolation), because, in the light of the gift of knowledge, creatures are rightly esteemed and ordered to the divine good, from which follows spiritual consolation, which begins in this life and will reach its fullness in the next.[190]

As for the fruits of the Holy Spirit, the gift of knowledge corresponds to a special certainty about supernatural truths, called *fides*, and a certain taste, delight, and fruition in the will, which is *gaudium* or spiritual joy.

Opposing Vices

St. Thomas, in the prologue to the question concerning sins against the gift of understanding, alludes to ignorance as a vice opposed to the gift of knowledge.[191] Let us see in what form.

The gift of knowledge, in fact, is indispensable to completely banish, by a certain divine instinct, the multitude of errors in matters of faith and morals that continually infect us because of our ignorance and mental weakness. Not only among uneducated persons, but even among theologians of note, in spite of the sincerity of their faith and the effort of their study, there are a multitude of opinions in matters of dogma and morals, which must necessarily be false except for one, because only one is the

---

[190] See STh II–II, q. 9 a. 4 c and ad 1.
[191] Ibid.

truth. Who will give us a sound and accurate criterion so as not to fall away from the truth in any of these intricate questions? In the universal and objective order there can be no problem, by virtue of the Magisterium of the Church, which is an infallible criterion of truth (for this reason, he who strictly adheres to the infallible Magisterium never errs). In the personal and subjective order, constant and flawless accuracy is something beyond human strength, even for the best of theologians. Only the Holy Spirit, through the gift of knowledge, can give it to us as a divine instinct, and so it happens that humanly uneducated and even illiterate persons astonish the greatest theologians by the certainty and depth with which they penetrate the truths of faith and the ease and accuracy with which they instinctively resolve the most intricate problems of morality. All false mystics are so precisely because of ignorance, contrary to this gift.

This ignorance can be culpable and constitute a real vice against this gift, and it can be so either by voluntarily occupying our spirit in vain or curious things, or even in human sciences without due moderation (allowing ourselves to be excessively absorbed by them and not giving place to the study of the most important science, which is that of our own salvation or sanctification), or by vain presumption, trusting too much in our own knowledge and our own lights, thus putting an obstacle to the judgments that we should form with the light of the Holy Spirit. This abuse of human science is the main reason why true mystics abound more among simple and ignorant people than among those who are too intellectual and wise according to the world. As long as they do not renounce their willful blindness and intellectual arrogance, it is not possible for the gifts of the Holy Spirit to act in their souls. Christ Himself warns us in the Gospel: "I thank thee, Father, Lord of heaven and earth, that thou hast hidden these things from the wise and understanding and revealed them to babes" (Matt. 11:25).

So ignorance, contrary to the gift of knowledge, which can and often does occur in men who are great and wise according to the world, is indirectly voluntary and guilty, constituting, by the same token, a true vice against the gift of knowledge.[192]

Means of Fostering This Gift

Apart from the means for the promotion of gifts in general (recollection, fidelity to grace, prayer, and so on), here are the principal ones pertaining to the gift of knowledge.

1. To consider the vanity of earthly things. We will never, by far, with our poor "little considerations,"[193] be able to approach the penetrating intuition of the gift of knowledge about the vanity of created things; but we can undoubtedly do something by seriously meditating on it with the discursive procedures within our reach. God does not ask of us at every moment more than what we can then give Him; and to him who does what he can on his part, God never denies His help for further progress.[194]

---

[192] I. G. Menéndez–Reigada, *The Gifts of the Holy Spirit and Christian Perfection*, 596–600.

[193] The expression, of an unsurpassable realistic force, is from St. Teresa, *Life*, 15, 14.

[194] The reading of certain works on this same subject can help in this task. The venerable Fray Luis de Granada wrote admirable pages in several of his works, and Fray Diego de Estella composed his famous treatise on the vanity of the world, which has not yet lost its freshness and relevance.

2. To become accustomed to relate all created
   things to God. This is another psychological procedure for gradually approaching the point of
   view in which the gift of knowledge will definitively place us. Let us not rest in the creatures: let
   us pass through them to God. Are not the created beauties a pale reflection of the divine
   beauty? Let us strive to discover in all things the
   trace and vestige of God, preparing the way for
   the superhuman action of the Holy Spirit.

3. To oppose energetically the spirit of the world.
   The world has the sad privilege of seeing all
   things (from the supernatural point of view) precisely the opposite of what they are. It is concerned only with the enjoyment of creatures,
   placing its happiness in them, with its back completely turned away from God. There is, therefore, no other attitude more contrary to the spirit
   of the gift of knowledge, which makes us despise
   creatures or use them only in relation to God
   and ordered toward Him. Let us flee from
   worldly gatherings, where false coinages totally
   contrary to the spirit of God are passed around
   as if they were legitimate currency. Let us renounce spectacles and amusements so often satu-
   rated, or at least influenced, by the unhealthy
   atmosphere of the world. Let us always be on our
   guard so as not to be surprised by the assaults of
   this crafty enemy, who tries to take our eyes off
   the great panoramas of the supernatural world.

4. To see the hand of Providence in the government
   of the world and in all the prosperous or adverse

events of our life. It is very difficult to place ourselves in this point of view, and we will never
fully attain it until the gift of knowledge, and
above all the gift of wisdom, is at work in us; but
let us strive to do what we can. It is a dogma of
faith that God takes care of us all with most loving Providence. He is our Father, who knows
much better than we do what is good for us, and
governs us with infinite love, even though we
often fail to discover His secret designs in what
He disposes or permits for us, for our relatives or
for the whole world.

5. To be very concerned about purity of heart. This
care will attract the blessing of God, who will
not fail to give us the gifts we need to achieve it
completely if we are faithful to His grace. There
is a very close relationship between the guarding
of the heart and the exact fulfillment of all our
duties and enlightenment from on high: "I understand more than the aged, for I keep thy precepts" (Ps. 119:100).

CHAPTER 13

The Gift of Understanding

THE GIFT OF understanding, the same as the gift of knowledge taken in a different aspect, is responsible for perfecting the theological virtue of faith. Let us study it carefully.[195]

Nature

The gift of understanding is a supernatural habit, infused by God with sanctifying grace, by which man's intelligence, under the illuminating action of the Holy Spirit, becomes apt for a penetrating intuition of revealed things and even of natural things ordered toward the ultimate supernatural end.

Let us slowly examine this definition to know the intimate nature of this great gift.

1. It is a supernatural habit infused by God with sanctifying grace. This is a generic element, common to all the gifts of the Holy Spirit. They are not simply transient actual graces, but true habits infused in the powers of the soul in grace to easily second the motions of the Holy Spirit Himself.

[195] See our *Theology of Christian Perfection*, n. 337–42.

2. By which man's intelligence. The gift of understanding resides, in effect, in the speculative understanding, previously informed by the virtue of faith, which it perfects to receive connaturally the motion of the Holy Spirit, which will put into action the given habit.

3. Under the illuminating action of the Holy Spirit. Only the divine Spirit can set in motion the gifts of His own name. Without His divine motion, the habits of the gifts remain idle, since man is absolutely incapable of acting on them even with the help of grace. They are direct and immediate instruments of the Holy Spirit, who is constituted, by the same token, as the motor and rule of the acts that proceed from them. From this comes the divine modality of the acts of the gifts (the only one possible by intrinsic requirement of the very nature of the gifts). Man can do nothing else, with the help of grace, than dispose himself to receive the divine motion by removing obstacles, remaining faithful to grace, humbly imploring that sanctifying action, and freely and meritoriously seconding the motion of the divine Spirit when it is actually produced.

4. Becomes apt for a penetrant intuition. This is the formal object of the gift of understanding, which points out the specific difference between it and the theological virtue of faith. The virtue of faith provides the created understanding with the knowledge of supernatural truths in an imperfect way, in the human way, which is proper and characteristic of the infused virtues when they act

by themselves (as we have already seen), whereas the gift of understanding makes man apt for the profound and intuitive penetration (superhuman, divine, suprarational) of these same revealed truths.[196] It is, quite simply, the infused contemplation of which the mystics speak (St. Teresa, St. John of the Cross, etc.), which consists in a simple and profound intuition of the truth (*simplex intuitus veritatis*).[197] The gift of understanding is distinguished from the other three intellective gifts (wisdom, knowledge, and counsel) in that its proper function is to penetrate deeply into the truths of faith in a plan of simple apprehension (that is, without passing judgment on them), while to the other intellective gifts correspond the right judgment on them. This judgment, if it refers to divine things, belongs to the gift of wisdom; if it refers to created things, it is proper to the gift of knowledge, and if it concerns the application to concrete and singular cases, it corresponds to the gift of counsel.[198]

5. Of revealed things and even of natural things ordered toward the ultimate supernatural end. It is the material object on which the gift of understanding is based. It embraces all that pertains to God, to man, and to all creatures with their origin and their end. This material object extends,

---

[196] "The gift of understanding falls upon the first principles of free knowledge (revealed truths), but in another way than faith. For it belongs to faith to attend to them; and to the gift of understanding, to penetrate them deeply" (STh II–II, q. 8 a. 6 ad 2).

[197] See STh II–II, q. 180 a. 3 ad 1.

[198] Ibid., q. 8 a. 6.

then, to everything that exists, but primarily to
the truths of faith, and secondarily to all other
things that have a certain order and relation to
the ultimate supernatural end.[199]

Necessity

No matter how much faith is exercised in the human or discursive
way (ascetical way), it can never reach its full perfection and development. For this, the influence of the gifts of understanding and
knowledge (mystical way) is indispensable.

The reason is very simple. Human knowledge is in itself discursive, by composition and division, by analysis and synthesis, not
by simple intuition of the truth. The infused virtues do not escape
from this general condition of human knowledge, since they function under the regime of reason and in our human way (asceticism).
But since the primary object of faith is God Himself—that is, the
"first truth manifesting itself (*veritas prima in dicendo*),"[200] which is
very simple—the complex discursive way of knowing it cannot be
more inadequate or imperfect. Faith is, in itself, an intuitive habit,
not a discursive one;[201] and for this reason the truths of faith can
only be grasped in all their purity and perfection (although always in
the chiaroscuro of mystery) by the intuitive and penetrating glance
of the gift of understanding—that is, when faith has been entirely
freed from all the discursive elements that impurify it and becomes
a contemplative faith. Then we arrive at pure faith, so insistently

[199] Ibid., a. 3.
[200] God can be considered as first truth in three ways: *in essendo*, that
is, in His very deity, or divine essence; *in cognoscendo*, that is, in His
infinite wisdom, which cannot deceive us; and *in dicendo*, that is, in
God's supreme truthfulness, which cannot deceive us.
[201] See STh II–II, q. 2 a. 1; *De veritate*, q. 14 a. 1.

inculcated by St. John of the Cross as the only means provided for the union of our understanding with God.

"By pure faith," writes a contemporary author, "is understood the adherence of the understanding to revealed truth, an adherence founded solely on the authority of God who reveals."[202] It excludes, therefore, all discourse. From the moment that reason comes into play, pure faith disappears, because an element foreign to its nature is mixed with it. Reason can precede and follow faith, but it cannot accompany it without denaturing it. The more there is of discourse, the less there is of adherence to truth by the authority of God, and consequently the less there is of pure faith.

From this it is evident that mystical or infused contemplation (caused by the gift of understanding and the other intellectual gifts) is necessary to arrive at the pure faith, without discourse, of which St. John of the Cross speaks; and, consequently, the necessity of mysticism for Christian perfection.[203]

Effects

The effects produced in the soul by the action of the gift of understanding are admirable, all of them perfecting the virtue of faith to the degree of incredible intensity and certainty that it reached in the saints. It manifests to them revealed truths with such clarity that, without completely unveiling the mystery to them, it gives them an unshakable certainty of the truth of our faith, to the point that it does not enter into their heads that there can be unbelievers or those undecided in matters of faith. This is seen experimentally in mystical

---

[202] Crisógono de Jesús Sacramentado, *Compendio de ascética y mística* (Bilbao: Mensajero, 1933), II, c. 2 a. 3 p. 104.

[203] We have explained all this at length in our *Theology of Christian Perfection*, n. 181ff, to which we refer the reader who wants more information on this very important point.

souls, who have developed this gift to an eminent degree; they would be willing to believe the opposite of what they see with their own eyes rather than doubt in the least any of the truths of the Faith.

This is a most useful gift for theologians (St. Thomas possessed it to an extraordinary degree), enabling them to penetrate into the depths of revealed truths and then to deduce, through theological discourse, the conclusions implicit within revelation.

The Angelic Doctor Himself points out six different ways in which the gift of understanding makes us penetrate into the deepest and most mysterious of truths of the faith.[204]

Firstly, it makes us see the substance of things hidden under the accidents. By virtue of this divine instinct, the mystics perceive the divine reality hidden under the eucharistic veil. Hence their obsession with the Eucharist, which becomes in them a true martyrdom of hunger and thirst. In their visits to the tabernacle they do not pray, they do not meditate, they do not discourse; they limit themselves to contemplating the divine Prisoner of Love with a simple and penetrating gaze, which fills their souls with infinite softness and peace: "I look at Him and He looks at me," as that simple villager possessed by the divine Spirit said to the holy Curé d'Ars.

Secondly, it uncovers the hidden meaning of the divine Scriptures. This is what the Lord did with His disciples on the road to Emmaus when He "opened their minds to understand the scriptures" (Luke 24:45). All mystics have experienced this phenomenon. Without discourse, without study, without the help of any human element, the Holy Spirit suddenly and intensely reveals to them the profound meaning of some sentence of Scripture and plunges them into an abyss of light. There they often find their motto, which gives meaning and direction to their whole life: St. Teresa's "I will sing forever the mercies of the Lord"

---

[204] See STh II–II, q. 18 a. 1.

(Ps. 89:1); "if anyone is little, let him come to me" (Prov. 9:4) of St. Teresa of Ávila; Sister Elizabeth of the Trinity's "praise of glory" (Eph. 1:6). For this reason, books written by men fall out of their hands, and they end up finding pleasure only in the inspired words, especially those that flowed from the lips of the incarnate Word.[205]

Thirdly, it shows us the mysterious meaning of the likenesses and figures. Thus St. Paul saw Christ in the rock that flowed with living water to quench the thirst of the Israelites in the desert, "And the rock was Christ" (1 Cor. 10:4), and St. John of the Cross discovers for us, with astonishing mystical intuition, the moral, anagogical, and parabolic meaning of a multitude of similarities and figures of the Old Testament that reach their full realization in the New Testament, or in the mysterious life of grace.

Fourthly, it reveals to us spiritual realities beneath the sensible appearances. The liturgy of the Church is full of sublime symbolisms that for the most part escape superficial souls. The saints, on the other hand, experience great veneration and respect for the "least ceremony of the Church," which fills their souls with devotion and tenderness.[206] It is the gift of understanding that makes them see, through those symbolisms and sensible appearances, the sublime realities that they contain.

Fifthly, it makes us contemplate the effects contained in the causes. Fr. Philipon writes:

> There is another aspect of the gift of understanding
> particularly sensitive in contemplative theologians.

[205] "I hardly find anything in books, except in the Gospel. That book is enough for me": St. Thérèse of the Child Jesus, *Novissima Verba*, May 15.

[206] "Against the least ceremony of the Church that anyone could see I would go, for her or for any truth of Sacred Scripture, I would put myself to death a thousand deaths": St. Teresa of Jesus, *Life*, 33, 5.

After the hard work of human science, everything is suddenly illuminated by an impulse of the Spirit. A new world appears in a principle or in a universal cause: Christ the Priest, the only Mediator of Heaven and earth; or the mystery of the Virgin Coredemptrix, spiritually carrying in her womb all the members of the Mystical Body; or, finally, the mystery of the identification of the innumerable attributes of God in His sovereign simplicity and the reconciliation of the unity of essence with the Trinity of Persons in a deity that infinitely surpasses the most secret investigations of every created gaze. So many other truths are there that deepen the gift of understanding effortlessly, tastefully, in the beatifying joy of an "eternal life begun on earth" in the very light of God.[207]

Finally, it makes us see the causes through the effects. Fr. Philipon continues:

In the reverse sense the gift of understanding reveals God and His almighty causality in His effects, without recourse to the long discursive procedures of human thought left to its own devices, but by simple comparative glance and intuition "in the manner of God." In the most imperceptible signs, in the least events of his life, a soul attentive to the Holy Spirit discovers in a single stroke the whole plan of Providence for him. Without dialectical reasoning about the causes, the simple sight of the effects of God's

---

[207] M. M. Philipon, *The Spiritual Doctrine of Sister Elizabeth of the Trinity*, c. 8 n. 7.

justice or mercy makes him glimpse the whole mystery of divine predestination, the "excessive love" (Eph. 2:4) with which God pursues souls in order to unite them to the beatifying Trinity. Through everything, God leads to God.[208]

Such are the principal effects that the action of the gift of understanding produces in the soul. It is already understood that, perfected by it, the virtue of faith reaches a very lively intensity. The veils of mystery are never completely torn in this life — "Now we see in a mirror dimly" (1 Cor. 13:12); but its unfathomable depths are penetrated by the soul with an experience so clear and intimate that it comes very close to intuitive vision. It is St. Thomas, a model of weight and serenity in everything he says, who wrote these astonishing words: "In this very life, the eye of the spirit having been purified by the gift of understanding, God can be seen in a certain way."[209]

On reaching these heights, the influence of faith extends to all the movements of the soul, illuminating all its steps and making it see all things through the supernatural prism. These souls seem to lose the instinct of the human in order to conduct themselves in everything by the instinct of the divine. Their way of being, of thinking, of speaking, of reacting to the slightest events of their own or other people's lives, baffles the world, which is incapable of understanding them. It could be said that they suffer from intellectual strabismus, seeing all things upside down from the way the world sees them. In reality, the twisted vision is that of the world. They have had the ineffable joy of having the Holy Spirit, through the gift of understanding, give them the true sense of Christ — "We

[208] Ibid.
[209] "In fue etiam vita, purgato oculo per donum intellectus, Deus quodammodo videri potest": STh I–II, q. 69 a. 2 ad 3.

have the mind of Christ" (1 Cor. 2:16) — which enables them to see all things through the prism of faith: "He who through faith is righteous shall live" (Rom. 1:17).

Beatitudes and the Fruits Derived from It

The sixth Beatitude refers to the gift of understanding: the gift of the pure of heart (Matt. 5:8).

In this Beatitude, as in the others, two things are indicated: one, by way of disposition or merit (the cleansing of the heart), and the other, by way of reward (the seeing of God); and in both senses it belongs to the gift of understanding. For there are two kinds of cleansing: that of the heart, by which all sins and disordered affections are expelled, accomplished by the virtues and gifts pertaining to the appetitive part; and that of the mind, purifying it from bodily phantasms and errors against faith, and this is proper to the gift of understanding, and as for the vision of God, it is also twofold: one, perfect, by which the very essence of God is clearly seen, and this is proper to Heaven; and another, imperfect, which is proper to the gift of understanding, by which, although we do not see directly and clearly what God is, we see what He is not; and the more perfectly we know God in this life the better we understand that He exceeds all that the understanding can comprehend.[210]

As for the fruits of the Holy Spirit — which are exquisite acts of virtue that come from the gifts — the gift of understanding has, as its proper fruit, *fides*, that is, the unshakable certainty of faith; and, as the ultimate and most finished fruit, *gaudium* (spiritual joy), which resides in the will.[211]

---

[210] See STh II–II, q. 8 a. 7.
[211] Ibid., a. 8.

Opposing Vices

St. Thomas devotes an entire question to the study of these vices.[212]
They are principally two: spiritual blindness and the dulling of the
spiritual sense.

The first is the total deprivation of vision (blindness); the second,
a notable weakening of vision (myopia). Both proceed from the sins
of the flesh (lust and gluttony), since there is nothing that impedes
so much the flights of the understanding, even naturally speaking,
as the vehement application to bodily things that are contrary to
it. Therefore lust, which carries with it a stronger application to
the carnal, produces spiritual blindness, which almost completely
excludes the knowledge and appreciation of spiritual goods; and
gluttony produces the dulling of the spiritual sense, which weakens man for that knowledge and appreciation, just as a sharp and
pointed object (a nail, for example) cannot easily penetrate a wall
if its point is obtuse and blunt.[213] A contemporary author writes:

> This blindness of the mind is what all lukewarm
> souls suffer from; for they have in themselves the
> gift of understanding; but, their minds being en-
> grossed in things here below, lacking interior recol-
> lection and the spirit of prayer, continually poured
> out through the spouts of the senses, without an
> attentive and constant consideration of divine
> truths, they never discover the sublime clarities en-
> closed in their darkness. This is why we often see
> them so deceived in speaking of spiritual things, of
> the refinements of divine love, of the beauty of the
> mystical life, of the heights of sanctity, which they

---

[212] Ibid., q. 15.
[213] Ibid., a. 3.

perhaps consider in some external works covered with the debris of their human views, considering as exaggerations and eccentricities the delicacies that the Holy Spirit asks of souls.

These are the ones who want to go the way of the cows, as it is vulgarly said: well rooted to the ground, so that the Holy Spirit cannot lift them up in the air with His divine breath. They are busy making little heaps of sand, with which they pretend to climb to Heaven. They suffer from this spiritual blindness, which prevents them from seeing the infinite holiness of God, the marvels that His grace works in souls, the heroism of abnegation that He asks of them to correspond to His immense love, the madness of love for Him whom love led to the madness of the Cross. They have little regard for venial sins, and perceive only the more serious ones, ignoring what they call imperfections. They are blind, because they do not take hold of that light that shines in the darkness (2 Pet. 1:19), and often they presumptuously pretend to guide others who are blind (Matt. 15:14).

He, therefore, who suffers from this blindness or myopia in his inner sight, which prevents him from penetrating the things of faith to the utmost, is not without guilt, because of the negligence and carelessness with which he seeks them, because of the annoyance that spiritual things cause him, loving more those things that enter him through his senses.[214]

---

[214] I. G. Menéndez–Reigada, *The Gifts of the Holy Spirit and Christian Perfection*, 593–94.

Means of Fostering This Gift

As we have already said several times, the working of the gifts of the Holy Spirit depends entirely on the divine Spirit Himself. But the soul can do much on its part by preparing itself, with the help of grace, for this divine action.[215] Here are the principal means:

1. To enliven the Faith, with the help of ordinary grace. It is well known that the infused virtues are perfected and developed by an ever more intense practice of them, and although it is true that, without leaving their human way of acting (ascetical way), they can never reach their full perfection and development, it is an excellent disposition for the Holy Spirit to come to perfect them with the gifts to do everything on our part by the ascetical procedures within our reach. It is a fact that, according to His ordinary Providence, God gives His graces to those who are best disposed to receive them.[216]

2. Perfect purity of soul and body. To the gift of understanding, as we have just seen, corresponds the sixth Beatitude, which refers to the pure in

---

[215] "Although in this work that the Lord does we can do nothing, but so that His Majesty may do us this mercy, we can do much by disposing ourselves" (St. Teresa of Jesus, *Fifth Dwelling*, 2, 1). The saint speaks of contemplative prayer of union, the effect of the gifts of understanding and wisdom.

[216] St. Teresa of Jesus says it beautifully in many ways: "As it does not remain because you have not disposed us, do not be afraid that your work will be lost" (*The Way*, 18:3). "Nice disposition is [the exercise of the virtues] so that I may do you all mercy" (*Third Dwelling*, 1, 5). "Oh, God help me, what true words and how the soul understands them that in this prayer sees it for itself! How we would understand them all if it were not for our fault! As we fail in not disposing ourselves ... we do not see ourselves in this mirror that we contemplate" (*Seventh Dwelling*, 2, 8).

heart. Only with perfect cleanliness of soul and body does the soul become capable of seeing God: in this life, in the chiaroscuro of faith profoundly illuminated by the gift of understanding, and in the next, with the clear vision of glory. Impurity is incompatible with both.

3. Interior recollection. The Holy Spirit is a friend of recollection and solitude. Only there does He speak to souls in silence: "I will allure her, and bring her into the wilderness, and speak tenderly to her" (Hos. 2:14). The soul that is a friend of dissipation and bustle will never perceive the voice of God in its interior. It is necessary to empty oneself of all created things, to withdraw into the cell of the heart in order to live there with the divine Guest until one gradually succeeds in never losing the presence of God, even in the midst of the most absorbing tasks. When the soul has done all it can to recollect itself and isolate itself from all that is not necessary, the Holy Spirit will do the rest.

4. Fidelity to grace. The soul must always be attentive not to deny the Holy Spirit whatever sacrifice He asks of it: "Harden not your hearts" (Ps. 95:8). We must not only avoid any fully voluntary fault, (which, however small, would grieve the Holy Spirit, according to the mysterious expression of St. Paul: "Beware of grieving the Holy Spirit of God"), but we must positively second all His divine motions until we can say with Christ: "I always do what is pleasing to him" (John 8:29). It does not matter that at times the sacrifices He asks of us seem to be beyond our strength. With the grace of

God, everything is possible—"I can do all things through Him who strengthens me" (Phil. 4:13)—and we always have recourse to prayer to ask the Lord in advance for the very thing He wants us to give Him: "Give me, Lord, what you command and command what you will."[217]

5. To invoke the Holy Spirit. But none of these means can be practiced without the help of the prevenient grace of the Holy Spirit Himself. We must therefore invoke Him frequently and with the greatest possible fervor, reminding our Lord of His promise to send the Spirit to us (John 14:16–17). The sequence of the feast of Pentecost (*Veni, Sancte Spiritus*), the hymn of Terce (*Veni, Creator Spiritus*) and the liturgical prayer of this feast (*Deus, qui corda fidelium*) should be, after the Our Father and Hail Mary, the favorite prayers of our interior souls. Let us repeat them many times until we obtain that *recta sapere* which the Holy Spirit will give us, and, in imitation of the apostles when they withdrew to the Upper Room to await the coming of the Paraclete, let us add to our supplications those of the Immaculate Heart of Mary, "With Mary, Mother of Jesus" (Acts 1:14), the most faithful Virgin[218] and heavenly spouse of the Holy Spirit.

---

[217] St. Augustine, *Confessions*, 1, 10, 29.

[218] The precious invocation of Our Lady's litany—*Virgo fidelis, ora pro nobis*—should be one of the favorite ejaculatory prayers of souls thirsting for God. The divine Spirit will be communicated to them in the measure of their fidelity to grace; and this fidelity is to be obtained through Mary, universal Mediatrix of all graces by the will of God Himself.

CHAPTER 14

The Gift of Wisdom

THE GIFT RESPONSIBLE for bringing the virtue of charity to its ultimate perfection is the gift of wisdom. Since charity is the most perfect and excellent of all the virtues, we can understand that the gift of wisdom will be, in turn, the most perfect and excellent of all the gifts. Let us study it with the attention it deserves.[219]

Nature

The gift of wisdom is a supernatural habit, inseparable from charity, by which we judge rightly of God and divine things by their ultimate and highest causes under the special instinct of the Holy Spirit, who makes us savor them by a certain connaturality and sympathy.

Let us slowly explain the definition to realize the true nature of this great gift.

1. It is a supernatural habit. That is to say, it is infused by God into the soul together with grace and the infused virtues, like all the other gifts.

2. Inseparable from charity. It is precisely the virtue that it comes to perfect, giving it a divine

---

[219] See our *Theology of Christian Perfection*, n. 368–73.

modality, which it lacks under the rule of human reason, even when enlightened by faith. Because of this connection with charity, the gift of wisdom (as a habit) is possessed by all souls in grace and is incompatible with mortal sin. The same is true of the other gifts.

3. By which we judge rightly. In this, among other things, it differs from the gift of understanding. What is proper to the latter, as we have already said, is a penetrating and profound intuition of the truths of faith in the form of simple apprehension, without passing judgment on them. Judgment is given by the other intellective gifts in the following way: concerning created things, the gift of knowledge, and concerning the concrete application to our actions, the gift of counsel. Insofar as it presupposes judgment, the gift of wisdom resides in the understanding as its proper subject; but since judgment, by connaturality with divine things, necessarily presupposes charity, the gift of wisdom has its causal root in charity, which resides in the will, and it is not a purely speculative wisdom, but also a practical one, since to the gift of wisdom belongs, in the first place, the contemplation of the divine, which is like the vision of principles; and in the second place, directing human acts according to divine reasons. By virtue of this supreme direction of wisdom by divine reasons, the bitterness of human acts becomes sweetness, and labor becomes rest.[220]

---

[220] See STh II–II, q. 45 a. 2; a. 3 c and ad 3.

4. From God. This difference is proper to the gift of wisdom. The other gifts perceive, judge, or act on things other than God. The gift of wisdom, on the other hand, falls primarily and most principally on God Himself, of whom it gives us a savory and experimental knowledge, which fills the soul with unspeakable softness and sweetness. Precisely by virtue of this ineffable experience of God, the soul judges all other things that pertain to it by the highest and supreme reasons, that is, by divine reasons; for, as St. Thomas explains, he who knows and tastes the highest cause par excellence, God Himself, is able to judge all things by His own divine reasons.[221] We will return to this when we point out the effects that this gift produces in the soul.

5. Of divine things. The gift of wisdom properly falls on divine things, but this is not an obstacle for its judgment to extend also to created things, discovering in them their ultimate causes and reasons that connect and relate them to God in the marvelous whole of creation. It is like a vision from eternity that embraces all created things with a scrutinizing gaze, relating them to God in their highest and deepest significance for their divine reasons. Even created things are contemplated by the gift of wisdom divinely. From this it is clear that the formal or primary object of the gift of wisdom contains the formal or primary object and the material object of faith; for faith looks primarily to God, and secondarily to other revealed

[221] See STh II–II, q. 45 a. 1.

truths. But it differs from it in that faith confines itself to believing, and the gift of wisdom experiences and savors what faith believes.[222]

6. For its ultimate and highest causes. This is the proper characteristic of all true wisdom. Wise, in general, is he who knows things by their ultimate and highest causes. Before reaching these heights there are various degrees of knowledge, both in the natural and supernatural realms, and so:

a) He who contemplates any thing without knowing its causes has a vulgar or superficial knowledge of it (e.g., the villager who contemplates an eclipse without knowing what it is due to).

b) The one who contemplates it, knowing and pointing out its proximate causes, has scientific knowledge (e.g., the astronomer before the eclipse).

c) He who can reduce his knowledge to the ultimate principles of natural being possesses philosophical or natural wisdom, which is called metaphysics.

d) He who, guided by the lights of faith, scrutinizes with his natural reason the revealed data in order to extract from them their

---

[222] Speaking of the sublime trinitarian experience of the soul reaching the heights of mystical union with God in the *Seventh Dwelling*, the effect of the very intense action of the gift of wisdom, St. Teresa writes: "O my God, how different it is to hear these words and believe them, than to understand in this way how true they are" (*Seventh Dwelling*, 1, 8).

intrinsic virtualities and deduce new conclusions possesses the highest natural wisdom
that can be attained in this life (theology),
radically connected already with the supernatural order.[223]

e) He who, presupposing faith and grace,
judges by divine instinct both divine and
human things according to their ultimate
and highest causes (that is, by their divine
reasons) possesses authentic supernatural wisdom, which is precisely that which gives the
soul the gift of wisdom in full operation.
Above this knowledge there is nothing higher
in this life. It is surpassed only by the Beatific
Vision and the uncreated Wisdom of God,
who is the divine Word.

Hence it is clear that the knowledge that the
intense action of the gift of wisdom gives the
soul is incomparably superior to that of all the
sciences, including sacred theology itself, which
already has something of the divine about it.
This is why sometimes there is the case of a simple and ignorant soul who lacks theological
knowledge acquired through study and yet possesses, through the gift of wisdom, a very

[223] It is well known that the habit of theology is entitatively natural,
because it proceeds from the natural discourse of reason by examining the data of faith and extracting from them their intrinsic virtues,
which are theological conclusions. But radically, that is, at its root, it
is or can be called supernatural, insofar as it starts from the principles
of faith and receives its illuminating influence throughout theological
discourse or reasoning (see STh I, q. 1 a. 6 c and ad 3).

profound knowledge of divine things that astonishes and amazes the most eminent theologians, as happened with St. Teresa and many other souls who had no formal education.

7. Under the special instinct of the Holy Spirit. This is proper and characteristic of the gifts of the same divine Spirit, which acquires its maximum exponent in the gift of wisdom because of the very loftiness of its object: God Himself and divine things. Man, under the action of the gifts, does not proceed by slow discourse and reasoning, but in a rapid and intuitive way, by a special instinct, which comes from the Holy Spirit Himself. Let us not ask the experimental mystics what reasons they have had for acting in this way or for thinking or saying this or that, for they do not know. They have felt it with a clairvoyance and certainty infinitely superior to all human discourse and reasoning.

8. Who makes us savor them by a certain connaturality and sympathy. This is another typical note of the gifts, reaching its highest perfection in wisdom, which is in itself a savory and experimental knowledge of God and divine things. Here, the word *wisdom* means both knowledge and taste. Souls who experience it understand very well the meaning of those words of the psalm: "O taste and see that the Lord is good!" (Ps. 34:8) They experience divine delights that push them to ecstasy and give them a foretaste of the ineffable joys of blessed eternity.

Necessity

The gift of wisdom is absolutely necessary for the virtue of charity to develop in all its fullness and perfection. Precisely because it is the most excellent virtue, the most perfect and divine of all, it is claiming and demanding, by its very nature, the divine regulation of the gift of wisdom. Left to itself—that is, managed by man in the ascetic state—it has to submit to human regulation, to the poor human way that man will necessarily imprint on it. Now, this human atmosphere becomes almost unbreathable; it chokes and suffocates it, preventing it from flying to the highest heights. It is a divine virtue that has wings to fly up to the sky, and it is forced to move at ground level: for human reasons, to a certain extent, without compromising much, with great prudence, with stunted meanness, and so forth. Only when it begins to receive the influence of the gift of wisdom—which gives it the atmosphere and divine modality that it needs by its own nature as a most perfect theological virtue—does charity, so to speak, begin to breathe freely, and, by a natural and inevitable consequence, it begins to grow and develop rapidly, carrying the soul with it, on wings as it were, through the regions of the mystical life and up to the summit of perfection, which it could never have reached via regulation in the ascetic, purely human state.

From this sublime doctrine two very important things can be deduced as inevitable corollaries. First: that the mystical state (that is, the habitual or predominant regime of the gifts of the Holy Spirit) is not only not something abnormal and extraordinary in the development of the Christian life, but is precisely the normal atmosphere that grace (divine form in itself) strains and demands so that it can develop all its divine virtualities through its operative principles (virtues and gifts), principally the theological virtues (faith, hope, and charity), which are absolutely divine in them-selves. The mystical should be precisely what is normal in every Christian, and it is, in fact, in every perfect Christian. Secondly: that an action of the gifts of the Holy Spirit in the human way, besides being impossible and absurd, would be completely use-less for perfecting the infused virtues, especially the theological virtues; the latter being superior to the gifts themselves by their very nature, the only perfection they can receive from them is the divine modality (proper and exclusive to the gifts), never a human modality (which the theological virtues already have, abandoned to themselves in the ascetic state and subjected to the human regulation of the poor soul imperfectly illuminated by the dark light of faith).[224]

Effects

Because of its own elevation and greatness and because of the sublime nature of the virtue that it directly perfects, the effects produced in the soul by the performance of the gift of wisdom are truly admi-rable. Here are some of the most important.

Firstly, it gives the saints the divine sense of eternity with which they judge all things. This is the most impressive of the effects of the gift of wisdom that appear outwardly. It could be said that the

---

[224] See STh I–II, q. 68 a. 8. The theological virtues, in fact, have as their direct and immediate object God Himself (believed, hoped for, or loved), while the gifts fall directly upon the infused virtues (that is, something very different from God) in order to perfect them. Therefore, it is evident that the theological virtues are, by their very nature, superior to the gifts themselves. On the other hand, these are superior to all the infused virtues, even the theological virtues, because of their divine modality (insofar as they are direct and immediate instruments of the Holy Spirit, not of the soul in grace, like the virtues). More briefly: the theological virtues are superior to the gifts because of their own theological nature, but the gifts are superior to them because of their divine modality.

saints have completely lost the instinct of the human and that this instinct has been replaced by the instinct of the divine, with which they see and judge all things. They see everything from the heights, from God's point of view: the small episodes of their daily life, as well as great world-historical events. In all things they see clearly the hand of God, who disposes or permits those things in order to obtain greater good. They never fix their attention on the immediate second causes; they pass through them, without stopping for an instant, up to the first cause, which rules and governs everything from above. They would have to do themselves great violence to descend to the points of view by which human meanness judges things. An insult, a slap, a slander hurled against them — and in the act they go back to God, who wills it or permits it, to exercise them in patience and increase their glory. They do not dwell for a moment on the second cause (the wickedness of men); they immediately go up to God and judge the fact from those divine heights. They do not call disgrace what men are accustomed to call it (sickness, persecution, death), but only what is disgrace in reality, because it is disgrace before God (sin, lukewarmness, infidelity to grace). They do not understand that the world can consider as riches jewels that shine a little brighter than the others. They see very clearly that there is no other true treasure than God and the things that lead us to Him. "What is this worth to me for eternity, to glorify God?" St. Aloysius Gonzaga used to ask himself. This is the only differential criterion of the saints to judge the value of things.

Among many other saints, this gift of wisdom shone to an eminent degree in St. Thomas Aquinas. The supernatural instinct with which he discovers in all things the divine aspect that relates and unites them to God is admirable. Such a great wisdom, so resounding, so universal in all that it touches, cannot be sufficiently explained by human wisdom, however elevated it may be supposed; it is necessary to think of the divine instinct of the gift of wisdom.[225]

In our days, the case of Sister Elizabeth of the Trinity is admirable. According to Fr. Philipon, who has studied so thoroughly the things of the famous Carmelite of Dijon, the gift of wisdom is the most characteristic of her mystical doctrine and of her life. He writes:

> Her soul was drawn by a sublime contemplative vocation to the very bosom of the Most Blessed Trinity, where she established her permanent abode, and from those divine heights she contemplated and judged all human things and events. The greatest trials, sufferings and setbacks did not succeed in disturbing for a moment the ineffable peace of her soul: everything slipped over her, leaving her "immobile and tranquil, as if her soul were already in eternity."[226]

Secondly, wisdom makes them live in an entirely divine way the mysteries of our holy faith. Let us listen to Fr. Philipon explaining these things admirably:

> The gift of wisdom is the real gift, the one that makes souls enter more deeply into the participation of divine knowledge. It is impossible to rise higher outside the Beatific Vision, which remains its superior rule. It is the gaze of the "Word breathing out Love" communicated to a soul that judges all things by their highest, most divine causes, by the supreme reasons, "in the manner of God."

[225] See A. Gardeil, *Los dones del Espíritu Santo en los santos dominicos* (Vergara: El Santísimo Rosario, 1907), c. 8.

[226] M. M. Philipon, *The Spiritual Doctrine of Sister Elizabeth of the Trinity*, c. 8 n. 8.

Introduced by charity into the intimacy of the
Divine Persons and in the heart of the Trinity, the
divinized soul, under the impulse of the Spirit of
love, contemplates all things from that center, an
indivisible point where they are presented to it as to
God Himself: the divine attributes, creation, redemption, glory, the hypostatic order, the smallest
events of the world. Insofar as it is possible for a
simple creature, his gaze tends to identify with the
angle of vision that God has of Himself and of the
whole universe. It is contemplation in the deiform
manner, in the light of the experience of the deity,
from which the soul experiences in itself the ineffable sweetness: *per quandam experientiam dulcedinis*
(STh I-II, q.112 a.5).

To understand this it is necessary to remember
that God cannot see things except in Himself: in their
causality. He does not know creatures directly in
themselves, nor in the movement of the contingent
and temporal causes that regulate their activity. He
contemplates them in His Word, in an eternal mode,
appreciating all the events of His Providence in the
light of their essence and their glory.

The soul, made a participant by the gift of wisdom in this divine way of knowing, penetrates with a
searching gaze into the unfathomable depths of the
Divinity, through which it contemplates all things
colored by the divine. It would seem that St. Paul was
thinking of these souls when he wrote those astonishing words: "The Spirit searches everything, even the
depths of God" (1 Cor. 2:10).[227]

[227] Ibid.

Thirdly, wisdom makes them live in society with the three Divine Persons, by means of an ineffable participation in their trinitarian life. Fr. Philipon writes again:

> Whereas the gift of knowledge takes an upward movement to raise the soul from creatures to God, and that of understanding, by a simple glance of love, penetrates all the mysteries of God from without and within, the gift of wisdom, so to speak, never goes forth from the very heart of the Trinity. Everything is presented to it in this indivisible center. The deiform soul thus cannot see things apart from their highest and most divine reasons. All the movement of the universe, down to the smallest atoms, falls under its gaze in the purest light of the Trinity and of the divine attributes, but in an orderly fashion, according to the rhythm in which things proceed from God. Creation, redemption, hypostatic order, even evil itself—everything appears to the soul as ordered to the greater glory of the Trinity. Rising, finally, in a supreme glance above justice, mercy, Providence, and all the divine attributes, the soul suddenly discovers all these uncreated perfections in their eternal source: in this deity, Father, Son, and Holy Spirit, who infinitely surpasses all our human conceptions, narrow and petty, and leaves God incomprehensible, ineffable, even to the gaze of the blessed and even to the beatific gaze of Christ; this God who is, at the same time, in His supereminent simplicity, unity, and Trinity, indivisible essence and society of three living Persons, really distinct according to an order of procession that in no way suppresses their consubstantial unity. The human eye would never have been able to discover

such a mystery, nor could the ear perceive such harmonies, nor the heart suspect such a Beatitude if by grace the Divinity had not bent down to us in Christ to make us enter into these unfathomable depths of God under the very direction of His Spirit.

The soul that has reached this point never leaves God. If the duties of its state so require, it gives itself externally to all kinds of work, even the most absorbing, with incredible activity; but "in the deepest center of its soul," as St. John of the Cross would say, it permanently feels the divine company of "its Three" and does not abandon them for a single instant. Martha and Mary have united in the soul in such an ineffable way that the prodigious activity of Martha in no way compromises the calm and peace of Mary, who remains day and night in silent and loving contemplation at the feet of the divine Master. The soul's life here on earth is already the beginning of a blessed eternity.[228]

Fourthly, it brings the virtue of charity to heroism. This is precisely the fundamental purpose of the gift of wisdom. Freed from its human bonds and receiving the divine air that the gift provides, the fire of charity soon acquires gigantic proportions. It is incredible how far the love of God reaches in souls worked by the gift of wisdom. Its most impressive effect is the total death to self. These souls love God with a most pure love, for His infinite goodness alone, without any mixture of human interest or motives. It is true that they do not renounce the hope of Heaven, indeed desiring it more than ever, but it is because in it they will be able to love God with even greater intensity and without any rest or interruption. If, by an

[228] Ibid.

impossibility, they could love and glorify God more in Hell than in Heaven, they would unhesitatingly prefer eternal torments.[229] It is the definitive triumph of grace, with the total death of selfishness itself. It is then that they begin to fulfill the first commandment of God's law as fully as possible in this poor exile.

In the aspect that looks to the neighbor, charity reaches, in parallel, a sublime perfection through the gift of wisdom. Accustomed to seeing God in all things, even in the smallest events, they see Him in a very special way in their neighbor. They love the neighbor with a profound tenderness, entirely supernatural and divine. They serve him with a heroic abnegation, full of naturalness and simplicity. They see Christ in the poor, in those who suffer, in the hearts of all their brothers, and they run to help Him with a soul full of love. They enjoy depriving themselves of the most necessary or useful things in order to offer them to their neighbor, whose interests they put before and prefer to their own, as they would those of Christ Himself. Personal selfishness in relation to one's neighbor is entirely dead. At times, the love of charity that burns in their hearts is so great that it overflows outwardly in divine follies that baffle human prudence and calculations. St. Francis of Assisi closely embraced a tree as a creature of God, wanting with it to join in an immense embrace the whole universal creation.

---

[229] This sentiment has been experienced by a great number of saints. See, for example, with what simple and sublime delicacy St. Thérèse of the Child Jesus expresses it: "One night, not knowing how to testify to Jesus that I loved Him and how vivid were my desires that He be served and glorified everywhere, I was overwhelmed by the sad thought that never again, from the abyss of Hell, would a single act of love reach Him. Then I told Him that I would gladly consent to see myself engrossed in that place of torments and blasphemies so that there, too, He would be loved eternally. I could not glorify Him in this way, since He desires nothing but our bliss; but when one loves, one is forced to say a thousand crazy things" (*History of a Soul*, c. 5 n. 23).

Finally, it gives to all the virtues the last trait of perfection and completion. It is a necessary consequence of the previous effect. Perfected by the gift of wisdom, charity makes its influence felt on all the other virtues, of which it is a true form (although extrinsic and accidental, as St. Thomas teaches). The whole of the Christian life experiences this divine influence. It is that something perfect and finished which the virtues of the saints have, and which we would seek in vain in less advanced souls. By virtue of this influence of the gift of wisdom through charity, all the Christian virtues are elevated and acquire a uniform modality, which admits innumerable nuances (according to the personal character and the kind of life of the saints), but all of them so sublime that it would not be possible to specify which of them is the most delicate and exquisite. With selfishness definitively dead, perfect in every kind of virtue, the soul settles on the summit of the mountain of holiness, where we read that sublime inscription: "Only the honor and glory of God dwells on this mountain" (Jer. 2:7).[230]

Beatitudes and the Fruits Derived from It

St. Thomas, following St. Augustine, attributes to the gift of wisdom the seventh Beatitude: "Blessed are the peacemakers, for they shall be called sons of God" (Matt. 5:9). He proves that it is appropriate in its two aspects: in terms of merit and in terms of reward.

As for merit ("the peaceful"), peace is nothing other than "the tranquility of order"; and to establish order (toward God, toward ourselves, and toward our neighbor) belongs precisely to wisdom.

As for the prize ("they shall be called sons of God"), we are precisely adopted sons of God because of our participation in and likeness to the only begotten Son of the Father, who is eternal Wisdom.[231]

---

[230] Expression that appears at the top of the "Mount of Perfection," painted by St. John of the Cross.

[231] See STh II–II, q. 45 a. 6.

Regarding the fruits of the Holy Spirit, these three are primary: charity, spiritual joy, and peace.[232]

Opposing Vices

Opposed to the gift of wisdom is the vice of stupidity or spiritual folly,[233] which consists in a certain dulling of judgment and spiritual sense that prevents us from discerning or judging the things of God according to God Himself by contact, taste, or connaturality, which is proper to the gift of wisdom. Even more regrettable is fatuity, which brings with it a total incapacity to judge divine things. Hence stupidity is opposed to the gift of wisdom as its opposite, and fatuity as its pure negation.[234] Menéndez-Reigada writes:

> We always suffer from this stupidity when we value the trifles of this world or judge that anything is worth anything other than the possession of the highest good or that which leads to it. Hence, if we are not saints, we must recognize that we are truly stupid, however much it may pain our self-love.[235]

When this stupidity is voluntary (because man has immersed himself in earthly things to the point of losing sight of or becoming incapable of contemplating the divine), it is a true sin, according to St. Paul: "The unspiritual man does not receive the gifts of the Spirit of God" (1 Cor. 2:14). Since there is nothing that brutalizes and animalizes man more than lust, to the point of submerging him

---

[232] Ibid., q. 70 a 3; q. 28 a. 1 and 4; q. 29 a. 4 ad 1.
[233] Ibid., q. 46.
[234] Ibid., a.1.
[235] I. G. Menéndez–Reigada, *The Gifts of the Holy Spirit and Christian Perfection*, 595.

completely in the mire of the earth, from lust principally comes spiritual stupidity or foolishness. Anger also contributes to it, which obfuscates the mind by strong bodily commotion, preventing it from judging righteously.[236]

Means of Fostering This Gift

Apart from the general means we already know (recollection, prayer life, fidelity to grace, frequent invocation of the Holy Spirit, profound humility, etc.), we can prepare ourselves for the working of the gift of wisdom with the following means, which are perfectly within our reach with the help of ordinary grace:

1. To strive to see all things from God's point of view. How many pious souls, and even those consecrated to God, see and judge all things from a purely natural and human point of view, if not entirely worldly! Their short-sightedness and spiritual myopia are so great that they never succeed in raising their eyes above purely human causes to see the designs of God in everything that happens. If they are disturbed, even inadvertently, they get angry and take it very badly. If a superior corrects some defect, they immediately brand him as demanding, tyrannical, and cruel. If he sends them something that does not suit their tastes, they lament his "lack of understanding," his "absent-mindedness," his complete "ineptitude to command." If they are humiliated, they cry out to Heaven. At their side, one must proceed with the same caution as when dealing

[236] See STh II–II, q. 46 a. 3 c and ad 3.

with a worldly person entirely devoid of supernatural spirit. No wonder the world is in such a
bad way when those who should be setting an
example are so often like this! It is not possible
for the gift of wisdom to ever act in such souls.
Such an imperfect and human spirit has completely suffocated the habit of the gifts. Until
they make a little effort to raise their eyes to
Heaven and, disregarding secondary causes, succeed in seeing the hand of God in all the prosperous or adverse events that happen to them,
they will always continue dragging their poor
and painful spiritual life on the ground. To learn
to fly, one must flap one's wings many times toward the heights, at whatever cost.

2. To combat the wisdom of the world, which is
foolishness and folly before God. The phrase, as
is well known, is from St. Paul (1 Cor. 3:19).
The world calls fools wise before God (1 Cor.
1:25), and, by an inevitable antithesis, those who
are wise before God are those whom the world
calls fools (1 Cor. 1:27; 3:18). Since the world is
full of this kind of foolishness, Sacred Scripture
itself tells us that "the number of fools is infinite"
(Eccl. 1:15). Fr. Lallemant writes:

> In fact, the majority of men have depraved
> tastes and can be with just reason called mad,
> since they do all their actions by placing their
> ultimate end, at least practically, in the crea-
> ture and not in God. Each one has some ob-
> ject to which he is attached and to which he
> refers all other things, having almost no

affection or passion except in dependence on that object, and this is to be truly mad.

Do we want to know whether we are of the number of the wise or of the foolish? Let us examine our likes and dislikes, whether before God and divine things, or between creatures and earthly things. Where do our satisfactions and displeasures come from? In what things does our heart find its rest and contentment?

This kind of examination is an excellent means of acquiring purity of heart. We should familiarize ourselves with it, examining frequently during the day our likes and dislikes and trying little by little to refer them to God.

There are three kinds of wisdom reprobated in Sacred Scripture (James 3:15), which are all true follies: earthly wisdom, which has no taste for anything but riches; animal wisdom, which has no taste for anything but the pleasures of the body; and diabolical wisdom, which sets its goal in its own excellence.

There is a madness that is true wisdom before God; to love poverty, self-contempt, crosses, persecutions, is to be mad according to the world, and yet wisdom, which is a gift of the Holy Spirit, is nothing other than this madness, which tastes only of what our Lord and the saints have tasted. But Jesus Christ has left in everything He touched in His mortal life, as in poverty, in abjection, on the

Cross, a sweet smell, a delicious taste; yet few souls have senses sufficiently subtle to perceive this smell and to savor this taste, which are altogether supernatural. The saints have run after the smell of these perfumes (see Songs 1:3), like St. Ignatius, who rejoiced at being despised; St. Francis, who loved abjection so passionately that he did things to make himself look ridiculous; St. Dominic, who was more at ease in Carcassonne, where he was usually mocked, than in Toulouse, where everyone honored him.[237]

3. Not to be too fond of the things of this world, even if they are good and honorable. Science, art, human culture, the material progress of the nations, and so on are good and honorable things in themselves, if they are properly channeled and ordered. If we give ourselves to these things with too much eagerness and ardor, they will not fail to do us serious harm. Our palate being accustomed to the taste of creatures, it will experience a certain dullness or stupidity in savoring the things of God, so superior in everything. Having allowed themselves to be absorbed by the disordered appetite for science, even sacred and theological science, many souls have been paralyzed in their spiritual life, a paralysis that is an irreparable loss; such souls lose the taste for the interior life, abandon or shorten prayer, allow themselves to be absorbed

[237] L. Lallemant, *The Spiritual Doctrine*, princ.4 c.4 a.1.

by intellectual work, and neglect the one thing necessary of which the Lord speaks to us in the Gospel (Luke 10:42). A great pity, which they will regret in the next world when it is beyond remedy! Fr. Lallemant continues:

> How different the judgments of God from those of men! Divine wisdom is folly in the judgment of men, and human wisdom is folly in the judgment of God. It is up to us to see with which of these judgments we want to conform our own. We must take one or the other as the rule for our actions. If we have a taste for praise and honor, we are mad in this matter, and we shall be as mad as we are fond of being esteemed and honored, just as, on the contrary, we have as much wisdom as we have love for humiliation and the cross.
>
> It is monstrous that even in religious orders one finds persons who like nothing more than what can make them pleasing to the eyes of the world; who have done nothing of what they have done during the twenty or thirty years of religious life except to approach the end to which they aspire; they have hardly any joy or sadness except in connection with this, or, at least, they are more sensitive to this than to all other things. Everything else that looks to God and perfection is insipid to them; they find no pleasure in it.
>
> This state is terrible and deserves to be mourned with tears of blood. For of what

perfection are these religious capable of? What fruit can they bear for the benefit of their neighbor? But what confusion they will experience at the hour of death when it will be shown to them that during the whole course of their life they have sought and tasted nothing but the glitter of vanity, as worldlings! If these poor souls are sad, say to them some word that will give them some hope of a certain aggrandizement, however false, and you will see them instantly change their countenance: their hearts will be filled with joy, as at the announcement of some great success or event.

On the other hand, as they have no taste for devotion, they do not qualify their practices as anything but trifles and the entertainments of weak spirits, and not only do they themselves govern themselves by these erroneous principles of human and diabolical wisdom, but they also communicate their sentiments to others, teaching them maxims altogether contrary to those of our Lord and of the gospel, of which they try to mitigate the rigor by forced interpretations conformable to the inclinations of corrupt nature, basing themselves on other misunderstood passages of Scripture, on which they build their ruin.[238]

4. Not to be attached to spiritual consolations, but to pass on to God through them. To such an

[238] Ibid.

extent does God want us for Himself alone, detached from everything created, that He wants us to detach ourselves even from the very spiritual consolations that He lavishes so abundantly at times in prayer. These consolations are certainly very important for our spiritual advancement, but only as a stimulus and encouragement to seek God with greater ardor. To seek them in order to dwell on them and savor them as the ultimate end of our prayer would be frankly wrong and immoral, and even to consider them as an intermediate end, subordinate to God, is something very imperfect, from which it is necessary to purify ourselves if we want to pass to perfect union with God.[239] We have to be ready and willing to serve God in darkness as well as in light, in drought as well as in comforts, in dryness as well as in spiritual delights. The God of consolations must be sought directly, not the consolations of God. The consolations are like the sauce or seasoning, which serves only to better take the strong foods, which truly nourish the organism; it alone does not nourish and can even spoil the palate, making insipid the convenient things when they are presented without it. The latter is bad, and must be avoided at all costs if we want the gift of wisdom to begin to act intensely in us.

[239] See St. John of the Cross, *Ascent of Mount Carmel* and *Dark Night*.

CHAPTER 15

Faithfulness to the Holy Spirit

WE HAVE SEEN in the preceding chapters how the Holy Spirit, together with the Father and the Son, is the sweet Guest of our soul, and we have also seen how He continually acts in us, whether by moving the habit of the infused virtues in the human way at the beginning of the spiritual life (the ascetical stage) or through the gifts in the divine way, until the faithful soul is brought to the summits of Christian perfection (the mystical stage).

But we cannot think that the Holy Spirit does not demand anything from the soul in exchange for His divine liberality and generosity. He demands from it a continuous fidelity to His divine motions, on pain of suspending or slowing down His action, leaving it stagnant in the middle of the road, with great danger even to its own eternal salvation.

For this reason we believe that our poor study, aimed at making known the Person and action of the divine Spirit in our souls, would be very incomplete, apart from its many other faults and imperfections, if we did not end it with a special chapter entirely dedicated to the exquisite fidelity with which the soul must unceasingly correspond to the sanctifying action of the Holy Spirit, who wants to lead it, in continuous ascending progression, to the highest summits of intimate union with God.

We will study the nature of fidelity to the Holy Spirit, its importance and necessity, its sanctifying efficacy and the concrete way to practice it.[240]

Nature

Fidelity, in general, is nothing other than loyalty, faithful adherence, the exact observance of the Faith that one owes to another. In feudal law it was the obligation of the vassal to present himself to his lord, to pay homage to him, and to be entirely obliged to obey him in everything, without ever putting up the slightest resistance.

All this applies to the highest degree when it comes to fidelity to the Holy Spirit, which is nothing more than loyalty or docility in following the inspirations of the Holy Spirit in whatever form they manifest themselves to us.

We call inspirations, St. Francis de Sales explains very well, all the attractions, movements, reproaches and inner remorse, lights, and knowledge that God works in us, foreseeing our heart with His blessings (see Ps. 20:4), by His paternal care and love, in order to awaken us, excite us, push us, and attract us to the holy virtues, to heavenly love, to good resolutions; in a word, to everything that leads us to our eternal good.[241]

Divine inspirations are produced in various ways. Sinners themselves receive them, impelling them to conversion; but, for the righteous, in whose soul dwells the Holy Spirit, it is perfectly connatural to receive them at every moment. The Holy Spirit, by means of them, enlightens our mind so that we can see what is to be done and moves our will so that we can and want to fulfill it, according

[240] See our *Theology of Christian Perfection*, n. 635–38; L. Lallemant, *Spiritual Doctrine*, princ. 4 c. 1 and 2; P. Plus, *Fidelity to Grace* (Barcelona: 1951); *Christ in Us* (Barcelona: 1943), 1.5.
[241] St. Francis de Sales, *Introduction to the Devout Life*, p. II c. 18.

to the words of the apostle: "God is at work in you, both to will and to work for his good pleasure" (Phil. 2:13).

For it is evident that the Holy Spirit always works according to His good pleasure. He inspires and works in the soul of the just when He wills and as He wills: "*Spiritus ubi vult spirat*" (John 3:8). Sometimes He enlightens only (e.g., in doubtful cases, to resolve the doubt); at other times He moves only (e.g., so that the soul may perform that good deed that it was already thinking of); at other times, finally, and this is the most frequent, He enlightens and moves at the same time.

Sometimes inspiration occurs in the midst of work, as if out of the blue, when the soul is completely distracted and oblivious to the object of inspiration. Many other times it occurs in prayer, in Holy Communion, in moments of recollection and fervor. The Holy Spirit rules and governs the adopted son of God both in the ordinary things of daily life and in matters of great importance. St. Anthony entered a church and, hearing the preacher repeat the words of the Gospel, "If you would be perfect, go, sell what you possess and give to the poor, and you will have treasure in heaven; and come, follow me" (Matt. 19:21), he immediately went home, sold all that he had, and withdrew into the desert.

The Holy Spirit does not always inspire us directly by Himself—sometimes He makes use of a guardian angel, a preacher, a good book, a friend—but He is always, ultimately, the main author of that inspiration.

Importance and Necessity

Faithfulness to the inspirations of the Holy Spirit is essential if we are to advance along the path of Christian perfection. In a certain sense, this is the fundamental problem of the Christian life, since on this rests our unceasing progress to the summit of the mountain of perfection or, otherwise, our remaining paralyzed at its very foot-hills. The almost sole concern of the soul must be to arrive at the most exquisite and constant fidelity to grace. Without this, all other procedures and methods that it attempts are irretrievably doomed to failure. The profoundly theological reason for this is to be sought in the present economy of grace, which is closely related to the degree of our fidelity.

Indeed, as we have already said above, the prior motion of actual grace is absolutely necessary if we are to perform any salutary act. It is in the supernatural order what the prior divine motion is in the purely natural order: something absolutely indispensable for a being in potency to be able to perform a supernatural act. Without it, it would be as impossible for us to perform the smallest supernatural act—even if we possess grace, virtues, and the gifts of the Holy Spirit—as it is to breathe without air. Actual grace is like divine air, which the Holy Spirit sends to our souls to make them breathe and live on the supernatural plane. Garrigou-Lagrange writes:

> Actual grace is constantly offered to us to help us in the fulfillment of the duty of each moment, just as air constantly enters our lungs to enable us to repair our blood, and just as we have to breathe in order to introduce into our lungs the air that renews our blood, in the same way we must desire positively and with docility to receive the grace that regenerates our spiritual energies to walk in search of God. He who does not breathe ends up dying of asphyxia; he who does not receive grace with docility will end up by dying of spiritual asphyxia. This is why St. Paul says: "We entreat you not to accept the grace of God in vain" (2 Cor. 6:1). It is necessary to respond to this grace and to cooperate generously with it. This is an elementary

truth which, practiced without faltering, would raise us to holiness.[242]

But there is still more. In the ordinary and normal economy of grace, God's Providence subordinates the subsequent graces that He will grant to a soul to the good use of the previous ones. A simple infidelity to grace can cut short the rosary of graces that God has successively granted us, causing us an irreparable loss. In Heaven we will see how the immense majority of frustrated sanctities (or rather, absolutely all of them) were spoiled by a series of infidelities to grace, perhaps venial in themselves, but fully voluntary, which paralyzed the action of the Holy Spirit, preventing Him from taking the soul to the summit of perfection.

Garrigou-Lagrange continues:

> The first grace of illumination, which effectively produces in us a good thought, is sufficient in relation to the generous voluntary consent, in the sense that it gives us not this act, but the possibility of performing it, only that, if we resist this good thought, we deprive ourselves of the actual grace, which would have inclined us effectively to consent to it. Resistance has the same effect on grace as hail on a blossoming tree that once promised abundant fruit: the blossoms are destroyed, and the fruit will not come in season. Effective grace is given to us in sufficient grace as fruit is given to us in the flower; of course, the flower must not be destroyed in order to reap the fruit. If we do not resist sufficient grace, actual efficacious grace is

---

[242] R. Garrigou–Lagrange, *Las tres edades de la vida interior* (Buenos Aires: Desclée, 1944), p. I, c. 3 a. 5.

given to us, and with its help we progress, with sure steps, along the path of salvation. Sufficient grace leaves us without excuse before God, and efficacious grace prevents us from glorying in ourselves; with its help we go forward humbly and generously.[243]

Fidelity to grace — that is, to the divine motions of the Holy Spirit — is therefore not only of great importance, but absolutely necessary and indispensable in order to progress along the path of union with God. The soul and its spiritual director should have no other obsession than that of arriving at a continuous, loving, and exquisite fidelity to grace. Fr. Plus writes:

> In reality, will not the history of our life be summed up many times in the history of our perpetual infidelities? God has magnificent plans for us, but we oblige Him to modify them continually. Such a grace that He was about to grant us, He has to suspend it because we have neglected to deserve it, and so correction is added to correction. What remains of the original plan?
>
> God lives in Himself, beforehand and eternally, that which He wants us to live in time. The idea He has of us, His eternal will for us, constitutes our ideal history, the great poem of our life. Our loving Father never ceases to inspire our consciousness with this beautiful poem. Each imperceptible vibration is a gift, a talent that I must receive, an impulse that I must follow, a beginning that I must finish and make worthwhile, and You know, O Father, the resistances,

[243] Ibid.

the misunderstandings, the perversions I introduce. At each resistance or misunderstanding, your Providence replaces with another poem (a poem diminished, but still magnificent) those and all the others whose inspiration I failed to follow.

There are souls that do not attain sanctity because one day, at a given moment, they did not know how to fully correspond to a divine grace. Our future sometimes depends on two or three affirmations or two or three denials that were agreed to be said but were not said, and on which hung generosity and failure without number.

To what heights we would not reach if we resolved to walk always at the same pace as the divine magnificence! Our cowardice prefers the steps of a dwarf.

Who knows to what mediocrities we condemn ourselves, and perhaps to worse things, for not having responded attentively to the calls from on high? We have heard the strange words of Jesus Christ to St. Margaret Mary about the danger of not being faithful, and this no less urgent one: "Be very careful never to let this lamp (your heart) go out, for if it goes out once, you will never again have fire to light it."

Have no false fear, but also no vain presumption. God's grace is not to be trifled with. It passes, and it is true that it returns many times, but it does not always return. If it returns, and we suppose that it comes with as much force as the first time, it finds the heart already weakened by the first cowardice; consequently, less armed to reciprocate, and then, God is less invited to give us another grace. What for, that it may suffer the same fate as the first? This wasted grace, this despised inspiration, this unspeakable "leaving on account" is a dangerous witness at the tribunal of God. The saints trembled at the thought of the evil caused by infidelity to divine inspirations.[244]

Sanctifying Efficacy

Leaving aside the sacraments, which, worthily received, are the fountain and source of grace, and whose sanctifying efficacy, all things being equal, is far superior to that of every other religious practice, there is no doubt that, among those things which depend on man's activity, the first place is held by perfect fidelity to the inspirations of the Holy Spirit. Let us listen to Bishop Saudreau on this:

> How could this divine grace not produce admirable things in the soul's docile heart? God, infinitely good and holy, desires nothing so much as to communicate His goods, to make His children partakers of His holiness and His happiness. His paternal gaze is constantly fixed on them, awaiting their goodwill, as if begging their consent to shower them with riches. His wisdom knows very well by what paths He will lead them to make them holy and happy. What guarantee, then, is there for those who always and in everything allow themselves to be guided by such a wise and loving guide? In these, the wave of His graces is ever increasing; at first, like an intermittent dew; then, like a little stream; then, like a current; finally, like a mighty river: At the same time that the graces are more abundant, they are also purer and more intense.[245]

[244] R. Plus, *Cristo en vosotros* (Barcelona: Libreria Religiosa, 1943), 169–70.
[245] A. Saudreau, *The Ideal of the Fervent Soul* (Barcelona: Eugenio Subirana, 1926), 108.

It is very useful to carry out seriously the test of not denying the Holy Spirit anything that He clearly asks of us. An ancient author affirms categorically that three months of perfect fidelity to all the inspirations of the Holy Spirit places the soul in a state that will surely lead it to the summit of perfection, and he adds: "Let anyone make the trial, for three months, of refusing absolutely nothing to God, and he will see what a profound change he will experience in his life."[246]

Fr. Lallemant writes:

> Our whole perfection depends on this fidelity, and it may be said that the summary and compendium of the spiritual life consists in observing attentively the movements of the Spirit of God in our soul and in reaffirming our will in the resolution to follow them docilely, using for this purpose all the exercises of prayer, reading, the sacraments and the practice of the virtues and good works....
>
> The end to which we should aspire, after having exercised ourselves for a long time in purity of heart, is that of being so possessed and governed by the Holy Spirit that He alone may be the one who leads and governs all our powers and senses and who regulates all our interior and exterior movements, abandoning us entirely to ourselves by the spiritual renunciation of our will and our own satisfactions. Thus we will no longer live in ourselves, but in Jesus Christ, by a faithful correspondence to the operations of His divine Spirit and by a perfect submission of all our rebelliousness to the power of grace....

[246] J. Mahieu, *Probatio caritatis* (Bruges: 1948), 271.

The reason why one arrives so late or never arrives at perfection is that in almost everything one follows only human nature and human sense. We never, or almost never, follow the Holy Spirit, whose role it is to enlighten, direct, and enkindle....

It can be truly said that there are but very few people who constantly keep to the ways of God. Many are constantly going astray. The Holy Spirit calls them with His inspirations; but, as they are indomitable, full of themselves, attached to their feelings, conceited of their own wisdom, they do not easily allow themselves to be led, they enter only rarely into the way and design of God and hardly remain in it, returning to their conceptions and ideas, which make them give way. Thus they advance very little, and death surprises them after they have taken but twenty steps, when they could have walked ten thousand if they had abandoned themselves to the guidance of the Holy Spirit.[247]

How to Practice It

The inspiration of the Holy Spirit is to the act of virtue what temptation is to the act of sin. By a simple footstep a man descends to sin: temptation, delectation and consent. The Holy Spirit proposes the act of virtue to the understanding and excites the will; the just person, finally, approves it and fulfills it.

On our part, three things are necessary for perfect fidelity to grace: attention to the inspirations of the Holy Spirit, discretion to know how to distinguish them from the movements of nature or of the devil, and docility to carry them out. Let us explain each of them a little.

[247] L. Lallemant, *The Spiritual Doctrine*, princ. 4 c. 2 a. 1 and 2.

1. Attention to inspirations. Let us often consider that the Holy Spirit dwells within us (1 Cor. 6:19). If we were to turn away from all things on earth and withdraw in silence and peace within ourselves, we would undoubtedly hear His gentle voice and the intimations of His love. This is not an extraordinary grace, but quite normal and ordinary in a Christian life seriously lived. Why, then, do we not hear His voice? For three main reasons:

First, because of our habitual dissipation. God is inside, and we live outside. "The inner man is soon gathered up, because he never pours himself out completely to the outside."[248] The Holy Spirit Himself expressly reminds us of this: "I will allure her, and bring her into the wilderness, and speak tenderly to her" (Hos. 2:14).

Here is a magnificent text by Fr. Plus insisting on these ideas:

> God is discreet; but He is neither timid nor impotent. He could impose Himself; if He does not do so, it is out of delicacy and to leave our initiative more room for action.
>
> But it cannot be imagined that the Lord is not a great lord; it cannot be that He does not have a very lively feeling of His supreme dignity.
>
> Let's suppose that where He wants to enter or work there is nothing but crazy worries, clatter of rattles, agitation, whirlwinds, wild colts, frenzy of speed, incessant displacements, inconsiderate search of nothingness that is stirred up; what is He going to ask for an audience for!
>
> God does not communicate with noise. When He discovers the interior of a soul obstructed by a thousand things, He is in no hurry to give Himself, to go and

---

[248] Thomas a Kempis, *Imitation of Christ*, II, 1.

lodge in the midst of these thousand trifles. It has its own love. It does not like to put itself on a par with trinkets. Sometimes, however, He takes it into His charge and, in spite of the inattention, imposes attention. He was not desired nor asked inside. He has entered and speaks. But in general He does not proceed in this way. It avoids a presence which, it is quite clear, was not wanted. If the soul is in a state of grace, it is evident that He resides in it, but He does not manifest Himself to it. Since the soul does not deign to notice Him, He remains unnoticed; since there are substitutes who are preferred to Him, the supreme good avoids being preferred in spite of everything. The more the soul pours itself into things, the less He insists.

If, on the contrary, He observes that someone gets rid of these trifles and seeks silence, God draws near to Him. This excites Him. He can manifest Himself, for He knows that the soul will hear Him. He will not always manifest Himself, nor will it be the most common thing to show Himself in a patent way; but the soul will certainly feel obscurely invited to ascend....

Another reason why the soul that aspires to fidelity must live a recollected life is that the Holy Spirit blows not only where He wills, but when He wills. The characteristic of interior calls, St. Ignatius observes, is that they manifest themselves to the soul without warning and as if they were barely audible. At any moment an invitation can come to us. At all times, therefore, it is necessary to be attentive; not, certainly, with anxious attention, but intelligent, in perfect harmony with the wise activity of a soul completely devoted to its duty.

Unfortunately, "most people live at the window," as Froissard said; concerned only with the commotion, the comings and goings of the street, they do not even glance at the man who, in silence, waits inside the room, often in vain, to be able to engage in conversation.[249]

A little further on, the same author adds:

How can recollection be achieved in practice? In the first place, it is necessary to set aside a fixed place for a determined time of prayer: one does not arrive at spontaneous, habitual prayer at all times, except by practicing a determined, prescribed prayer at a fixed time and hour. It is up to each one to consult his particular grace, the circumstances in which his obligations place him and the advice of his spiritual director.

Once the exercises of prayer have been determined, it is necessary to train oneself in habitual recollection, in a certain exterior silence of action or word and, above all, in interior silence. A few simple principles sum it all up: Speak only when the word is better than silence.

Avoid the rush, the natural haste. The quickest thing to do when in a hurry is not to hurry. As a great surgeon used to say when he was about to perform an urgent operation: "Gentlemen, let us go slowly; we cannot waste a moment." Who does not remember the reproaches that Bishop Dupanloup used to address to himself at every retreat: "I have a terrible activity.... I will always take more time than necessary to do something." At the end of his life: "I have not wasted enough time, I have done too many things,

---

[249] P. Plus, *Fidelity to Grace*, 59ff.

too many small things at the expense of big things," and he always repeated the same thing: "Let us not give up the interior life for anything; always the interior life first of all." Did he not dream for some time of retiring to the Grande Chartreuse?[250]

Second, because of our lack of mortification. We are still too carnal and do not esteem and savor only the things that are external and pleasing to the senses, and, as St. Paul says, "the animal man does not perceive the things of the Spirit of God" (1 Cor. 2:14). The spirit of mortification is absolutely indispensable. It is necessary to practice the famous *agere contra*, which St. Ignatius of Loyola inculcated so much.

Third, because of our disordered affections. "If a person is not completely free from creatures, he will not be able to tend freely to divine things. For this reason there can be found so few contemplatives, because few attain this total detachment from creatures and passing things.[251] Two things, then, must be practiced in order to hear the voice of God: to detach oneself from all earthly affections and to attend positively to the divine Guest of our souls. The soul must always be in an attitude of humble expectation: "Speak, O Lord, for your servant is listening" (1 Sam. 3:10).

2. Discretion of spirits. Discernment or discretion of spirits is of great importance in the spiritual life, in order to know which spirit is moving us at a given moment. Here are some of the most important criteria for knowing the divine inspirations and distinguishing them from the movements of nature itself or of the devil:

[250] Ibid.
[251] Thomas a Kempis, *Imitation of Christ*, III, 31.

First, the sanctity of the object. The devil never impels to virtue; nor does nature usually do so when it is an uncomfortable and difficult virtue.

Second, conformity to our own state. The Holy Spirit cannot impel a Carthusian to preach, nor a contemplative nun to care for the sick in hospitals.

Third, peace and tranquility of heart. St. Francis de Sales says: "One of the best signs of the goodness of all inspirations, and particularly of the extraordinary ones, is the peace and tranquility in the heart of the one who receives them; because the divine Spirit is, indeed, violent, but with sweet, soft, and gentle violence. It appears like a mighty wind (Acts 2:2) and like heavenly lightning, but it does not overthrow or disturb the apostles; the fright that its noise causes in them is momentary and is immediately accompanied by a sweet security."[252] The devil, on the contrary, makes a fuss and fills them with restlessness.

Fourth, humble obedience: "Everything is safe in obedience, and everything is suspect outside it.... He who says he is inspired and refuses to obey his superiors and follow their advice is an impostor."[253] Witnesses of this are a great number of heretics and apostates who claimed to be inspired by the Holy Spirit or to enjoy a special charism.

Fifth, the judgment of the spiritual director. In things of little importance that happen every day, there is no need for long deliberation, but simply to choose what seems most in accord with the divine will, without scruples or worries of conscience; but in doubtful things of greater importance, the Holy Spirit always consults with superiors or the spiritual director.

[252] St. Francis de Sales, *Treatise on the Love of God*, 8, 12.
[253] Ibid., 6, 13.

3. Docility in execution. It consists in following the inspiration of grace at the very moment it occurs, without making the Holy Spirit wait a second.[254] He knows better than we do what is best for us; let us therefore accept what He inspires us to do and let us carry it out with a joyful and hardened heart. The soul must always be ready to do the will of God at all times: "Teach me to do thy will, for thou art my God" (Ps. 142:10).

Nature, dissatisfied with this, will place a triple obstacle in our way:

First, the temptation to procrastinate. It is like saying to the Holy Spirit: "Excuse me for today; I will do it tomorrow."

Because God generally puts into His requests an infinite discretion, in which consists the gentleness of His ways, we come to forget how hateful it is to keep the Sovereign Majesty waiting. We know that we must respond immediately to an order from the Vicar of Christ on earth! Shall we allow ourselves to be negligent because it is God Himself who commands? Precisely because He is so delicate in requesting our fidelity, great delicacy on our part should make us fly to serve Him, as do the saints.

Many souls reach the end of their lives without ever or almost never having consented to the Holy Spirit being their absolute owner. They have always prevented Him from entering, they have always made Him wait. At the hour of death they will see it clearly, but then it will be too late: there will be no more room for "tomorrow without fail," for continuous procrastination. Time is over and we enter eternity. Let us often think of the laments of that last hour for not having responded immediately to the inspirations of grace,

---

[254] It is understood that this refers only to cases in which the divine inspiration is absolutely clear and manifest. In doubtful cases it would be necessary to reflect, applying the rules of discernment or consulting with the spiritual director.

for having made the One who would have wanted to elevate us so much wait too long.

Second, theft of the will. Sometimes we proclaim or confess our own cowardice. We are afraid of the sacrifice that is asked of us. It is the fear that we all feel when it is a question of executing ourselves (every execution carries with it the death of something in us, it is always a "capital execution"). Nature protests, lamenting beforehand the generosities to which it will have to consent. Rivière cried:

> My God! Remove from me the temptation to holiness. Be content with a pure and patient life, which I will try with all my efforts to offer you. Do not deprive me of the delightful joys that I have known, that I have loved so much and that I so much desire to live again. Make no mistake, I do not belong to the precise class. Do not tempt me with impossible things.[255]

Here we have a vivid description, in a not at all vulgar soul, of the fear of total surrender, the inclination to beat around the bush, the very explainable prurience to avoid the obstacle instead of overcoming it.

However, if only we suspected what reward awaits total and generous surrender! We all know the story of the Indian beggar that Rabindranath Tagore tells. It is the story of many lives:

> I was walking, begging from door to door on my way to a village, when your golden chariot appeared in the distance, like a radiant dream, and I admired the king of kings.
>
> The carriage stopped. You looked at me and got out smiling. I felt the luck of my life arrive. Suddenly

---

[255] S. Rivière, *A la trace de Dieu* (Paris: Gallimard, 1948), 279.

you stretched out your right hand to me and said: "What are you going to give me?"

Ah, what joke was this, a king reaching out his hand to a beggar to beg? I was confused and perplexed. Finally, I took out of my saddlebags a grain of wheat and gave it to you. But great was my surprise when, as the day was drawing to a close and I emptied my sack, I found a tiny nugget of gold among the handful of common grains. Then I wept bitterly and said to myself: "What a pity I did not have the hunch to give it all to you!"[256]

Third, the eagerness to get back what we have given. If only, after having handed over the measly grain of wheat or the meager stock of our saddlebags, we did not try to get them back! It is the eternal story of the children who, having offered their goodies in front of the crib, as soon as we turn our backs they try to get them back to "savor their sacrifice."

The Doge of Venice, upon taking office, threw a gold ring into the sea to symbolize the marriage of the republic with the ocean. But it is said that, as soon as the feast was over, the divers were in charge of recovering it.

That's how we all are. Who, without much investigation, will not find similar examples in their moral conduct? Are we not accustomed to being subjected to subtractions in our burnt offerings, to wait avidly and immediately for the reward after the offering of our best sacrifices? Eternal misery of our condition! We must humble ourselves for it, but not be discouraged, and do all we can so that the credit of our selfishness may be as small as possible.

[256] R. Tagore, *Selected Poems* (Buenos Aires: Longseller, 2005), 65.

How to Repair Our Infidelities

After the supreme misfortune of eternal damnation, there is no greater misfortune than the misuse of divine graces. But just as eternal misfortune is absolutely irreparable, so infidelities to grace can be repaired in whole or in part while we still live in this world.[257] In a prayer spread among some religious communities, this triple petition to Divine Mercy is formulated:

> My God, have mercy on me and be merciful and liberal enough to make me make reparation, before my death, for all the loss of graces that I have had the misfortune or folly to bring upon myself.
>
> Make me reach the degree of merit and perfection to which you wanted to bring me according to your first intention, and which I have had the misfortune to frustrate with my infidelities.
>
> Also be good enough to make reparation to souls for the loss of grace that has been caused by my fault.[258]

Nothing is more reasonable than such requests. God can, if we ask Him, increase the prepared graces for a soul; and if it proves faithful in these new divine advances, such an increase can compensate for previous losses. To the one who did not face adversity, the Lord can send him others in the future: those he would have had if he had always been loyal and those destined to replace the ones that did not bear fruit. The occasions of sacrifices can also be multiplied to replace the sacrifices that were refused. The graces of light can

---

[257] A. Saudreau, *The Ideal of the Fervent Soul* (Barcelona: Eugenio Subirana, 1926), 128ff.

[258] Lallemant teaches that we should address these three petitions to God many times.

be more abundant, the will can receive more strength, and God can communicate a firmer, more intense and deepened love. These supplements are not above the power of God, nor are they contrary to His justice. It is true, most certainly, that the unfaithful soul does not deserve them; but fervent and persevering prayer — to which God has promised everything (Matt. 7:7–11) — can infallibly obtain them.

How else could it be explained that great sinners have become great saints? Their past sins were an occasion to rise to greater virtue. The desire to make reparation for them induced them to practice great austerities and to redouble their fervent love for God. The tears of St. Peter, which continued to be shed throughout his life, would not have flowed so copiously and, therefore, produced such numerous acts of love, if he had not denied his Master so cowardly. Our Lord told St. Margaret of Cortona that her penances had so erased her nine years of disorder that in Heaven He would place her in the choir of virgins. These and many other examples teach us that we must never be discouraged by our sins and past infidelities; but also that it is not enough to deplore them: it is necessary to repair and expiate them. If the train of our life is late approaching the station of arrival, it is evident that we will arrive there with an irreparable delay unless we intensely increase our speed, dedicating what remains of our life to a total and absolute surrender to the ever more pressing demands of intimate union with God.

The atonement makes God more favorable, attracts graces much more abundant and powerful, removes from the soul the impediments placed by sin, which prevent the perfect exercise of the virtues. In this way it not only makes reparation for previous faults, but by it the soul is elevated in virtue much more than if it had not sinned. St. Paul wrote in his Letter to the Romans these consoling words: "In everything God works for good with those who love him, who are called according to his purpose" (Rom. 8:28); the genius of St. Augustine dared to add *etiam peccata*, even sins themselves.

If, on the contrary, we do not take to heart to atone for our faults and make reparation for the abuses committed against the graces and inspirations received from divine goodness, the Lord will give to other faithful souls the graces that we so foolishly and madly despise. He expressly warns us in the parable of the minas: " 'Take the pound from him, and give it to him who has the ten pounds.' (And they said to him, 'Lord, he has ten pounds!') 'I tell you, that to every one who has will more be given; but from him who has not, even what he has will be taken away' " (Luke 19:24–26).

It is very consoling to think that, even after having been disloyal, it is possible to recover what has been lost by being generous with God. Undoubtedly, if we do not make an effort to redouble our fervor, taking occasion precisely from our past infidelities, we will not make up for lost time or reach the degree of perfection to which God wanted to raise us, just as the train cannot make up for the delay suffered in the middle of its journey if the engineer does not take care to speed up the train before its arrival at its terminus.

Some distrustful hearts imagine that they can no longer hope to rise to the degree of fervor from which they fell by their continued unfaithfulness to grace. They know very poorly divine long-suffering and mercy. Countless are the texts of Sacred Scripture that expressly inculcate this in us: "let the wicked forsake his way, and the unrighteous man his thoughts; let him return to the Lord, that he may have mercy on him, and to our God, for he will abundantly pardon. For my thoughts are not your thoughts, neither are your ways my ways, says the Lord. For as the heavens are higher than the earth, so are my ways higher than your ways" (Isa. 55:7–9). This means that God's mercy, "that mercy which fills the universe" (Ps. 33:5), far surpasses the idea that the rickety intelligence of men can be formed from it.

Even those who have abused the most, because they have received the most, should have this confidence, for if they have received so much, it is because God preferred them, and it only remains for them to return to what they were. As St. Paul teaches, "the gifts and the call of God are irrevocable" (Rom 11:29). Undoubtedly, the divine designs are suspended when man puts obstacles in their way; but God does not revoke His choice. Remove the obstacles and the original plans of Providence will be realized. Those who have tasted the gifts of God, those who have received a special vocation to holiness, those who have been favored by mystical graces, may have lost by their infidelity such immense favors; but God, who has treated them as privileged, is always ready to enrich them with greater graces, if they want to atone generously for their faults and past errors.

We must therefore foster in ourselves the holy ambition to acquire for eternity this wealth of glory, or rather, since our happiness will consist in the love and possession of the beloved God, we must strive to acquire the great sum of love that God predestined for us when He created us. However great our infidelities may have been up to now, let us believe with firm confidence that we can, with divine help, repair and recover what has been lost. But let us understand very well that, in order to achieve this desirable result, it is necessary to be generous to the utmost, and we must begin our task today, without further suicidal delays. The day is already waning (Luke 24:29) and night is approaching, in which no one can work (John 9:4); or, if we prefer, the shadows of the night of this life are already dissipating and the first lights of eternity are already dawning on the near horizon. We must hurry so as not to arrive too late.

Consecration to the Holy Spirit

There is a magnificent formula, widespread among many religious communities, to express to the Holy Spirit our total surrender and perfect consecration to His Divine Person. Of course, it is not enough to recite a prayer, no matter how sublime it may be; it is necessary to live that perfect consecration that we want to express with it. But there is no doubt that, reciting and savoring slowly the magnificent formula that we collect below, we will end up achieving from the Divine Mercy a perfect attunement between our life and what is expressed by that fervent prayer. Here it is:

> O Holy Spirit, divine bond that unites the Father with the Son in an ineffable and very close bond of love! Spirit of light and truth, deign to pour out all the fullness of your gifts upon my poor soul, which I solemnly consecrate to you forever, so that you may be its preceptor, its director, and its teacher. I humbly ask of You fidelity to all your desires and inspirations and complete and loving surrender to Your divine action.
>
> O Creator Spirit! Come, come, and work in me the renewal for which I ardently sigh; renewal and transformation such that it will be like a new creation, all of grace, purity, and love, with which I will truly begin the entirely spiritual, heavenly, angelic, and divine life that my Christian vocation demands.
>
> Spirit of holiness, grant my soul the touch of your purity, and it will be whiter than snow! Sacred source of innocence, of candor and virginity, give me to drink of your divine water, quench the thirst for purity that burns me, baptizing me with that Baptism of fire whose divine baptistery is your

divinity, you yourself! Envelop my whole being with its purest flames. Destroy, devour, consume in the ardors of pure love everything in me that is imperfect, earthly, and human, everything that is not worthy of you.

May your divine anointing renew my consecration as a temple of the whole of the Most Holy Trinity and as a living member of Jesus Christ, to whom, with even greater perfection than hitherto, I offer my soul, body, powers, and senses with all that I am and have.

Wound me with love, O Holy Spirit, with one of those intimate and substantial touches, so that, like a flaming arrow, it may wound and pierce my heart, making me die to myself and to all that is not the Beloved, a happy and mysterious transit that only you, O divine Spirit, can bring about, and which I long for and humbly ask for.

Like a chariot of divine fire, snatch me from earth to Heaven, from myself to God, so that from today I may dwell in that Paradise which is His heart.

Instill in me the true spirit of my vocation and the great virtues that it demands and that are a sure pledge of holiness: love of the cross and of humiliation, and contempt for all that is transitory. Give me, above all, a most profound humility and a most holy hatred of myself. Ordain in me charity and intoxicate me with the wine that begets virgins.

May my love for Jesus be most perfect, to the point of complete alienation of myself, to that heavenly insanity that makes me lose the human sense of all things, to follow the lights of faith and the impulses of grace.

Receive me, then, O Holy Spirit; may I give myself wholly and completely to you. Possess me, admit me into the most chaste delights of your union, and in it may I faint and expire of pure love on receiving your kiss of peace. Amen.[259]

---

[259] We do not know who the author of this precious prayer is. Fr. Arintero used to spread it to select souls. Fr. Arintero was the founder of the "La Vida Sobrenatural" magazine and died in Salamanca on February 20, 1928, in the odor of sanctity. The cause for his beatification has already been introduced in Rome. We do not know if he wrote the Consecration to the Holy Spirit himself or if he received it from one of the great souls he knew how to lead to the summits of sanctity.

About the Author

Fr. Antonio Royo Marín, O.P. (1913–2005) was a master of the spiritual life, a brilliant orator, a professor, and a renowned author. For his excellence in study and service to the Church, Fr. Marín was awarded the medal *Pro Ecclesia et Pontifice* by St. John Paul II.

Sophia Institute

SOPHIA INSTITUTE IS a nonprofit institution that seeks to nurture the spiritual, moral, and cultural life of souls and to spread the gospel of Christ in conformity with the authentic teachings of the Roman Catholic Church.

Sophia Institute Press fulfills this mission by offering translations, reprints, and new publications that afford readers a rich source of the enduring wisdom of mankind.

Sophia Institute also operates the popular online resource CatholicExchange.com. *Catholic Exchange* provides world news from a Catholic perspective as well as daily devotionals and articles that will help readers to grow in holiness and live a life consistent with the teachings of the Church.

In 2013, Sophia Institute launched Sophia Institute for Teachers to renew and rebuild Catholic culture through service to Catholic education. With the goal of nurturing the spiritual, moral, and cultural life of souls, and an abiding respect for the role and work of teachers, we strive to provide materials and programs that are at once enlightening to the mind and ennobling to the heart; faithful and complete, as well as useful and practical.

Sophia Institute gratefully recognizes the Solidarity Association for preserving and encouraging the growth of our apostolate over the course of many years. Without their generous and timely support, this book would not be in your hands.

www.SophiaInstitute.com
www.CatholicExchange.com
www.SophiaInstituteforTeachers.org

Sophia Institute Press is a registered trademark of Sophia Institute.
Sophia Institute is a tax-exempt institution as defined by the
Internal Revenue Code, Section 501(c)(3). Tax ID 22-2548708.